PLUTARCH

LIFE OF PERICLES

A companion to the Penguin translation from
The Rise and Fall of Athens,
translated by Ian Scott-Kilvert,
published in the Penguin Classics

Introduction and Commentary by

A.J. Podlecki

Bristol Classical Press

This impression 2003
This edition first published in 1987 by
Bristol Classical Press
an imprint of
Gerald Duckworth & Co. Ltd.
90-93 Cowcross Street
London EC1M 6BF
inquiries@duckworth-publishers.co.uk
www.ducknet.co.uk

Published with assistance from The Centenary Fund of the
Society for the Promotion of Hellenic Studies.

A catalogue record for this book is available
from the British Library

ISBN 0 86292 237 2

Cover illustration: Pericles, after Roman copies of a portrait
statue by the mid-fifth century sculptor Cresilas, British and
Vatican Museums. (Drawing by Jean Bees)

Contents

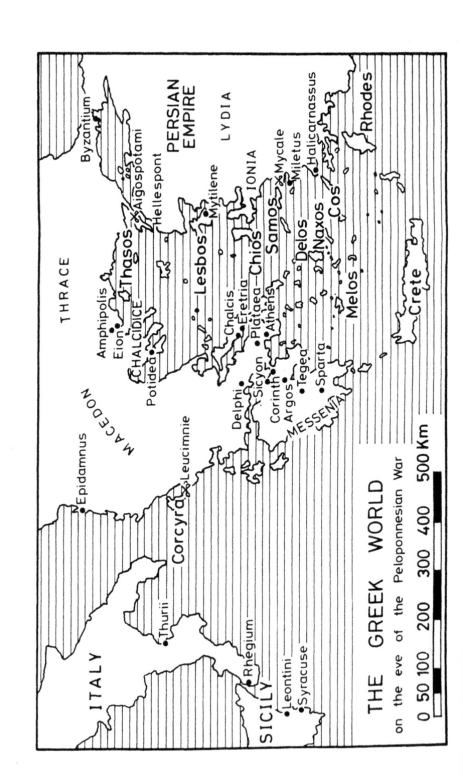

THE GREEK WORLD
on the eve of the Peloponnesian War

0 50 100 200 300 400 500 Km

Introduction

1. PLUTARCH'S LIFE AND WRITINGS

Plutarch was a native of Chaeronea, a town in Boeotia which was the site of Philip's victory over the Athenians and Thebans in 338 B.C. A birth-date between 45 and 50 A.D. can be inferred from Plutarch description of himself as a 'youth' when Nero visited Greece in 67 A.D.; he died about 120 A.D. His family was long-established and fairly well-to-do: local gentry, in fact. Plutarch went to Athens for part of his education where he studied under the Egyptian philosopher, Ammonius. While still a young man, he officially represented his native city on an embassy to the Roman governor of Achaea and later also to Rome itself, where he probably returned several times in the period between 75 and 90 A.D. At Rome he made influential friendships, which led to a grant of Roman citizenship; since he was also, at some stage in his career, made an honorary Athenian citizen, he was able to claim citizenship in both the leading intellectual capitals of his day. Although he travelled widely through the rest of Greece, and beyond, he must have revisited Athens many times, and this gave him ample opportunity to become thoroughly familiar with her monuments and topography. Above all, he acquired a deep respect for her history and traditions, and an admiration for the record of her accomplishments. For the most part, however, Plutarch was content to stay in Chaeronea, where, in addition to holding various priestly and political offices, he undertook the founding of a school, married, fathered five children—and wrote voluminously.

His writings are generally divided into two groups, the *Lives* (23 pairs of *Parallel Lives*, of which the first pair does not survive, and four separate *Lives*) and the *Moralia*, sixty or so essays on a wide range of topics, not only religion, philosophy and ethics, but politics, natural science and psychology, and a few that defy classification, such as *Greek Questions*, *Roman Questions* and *Table Talk*. In addition, Plutarch wrote a great deal that has not survived. A Plutarch specialist, Konrad Ziegler, estimates that what we have represents only 'approximately half of what Plutarch wrote in the course of his long life.'

Plutarch himself tells us (*Per.* 2), that his *Life of Pericles* came at the beginning of his tenth 'book' (each 'book' in Plutarch's own edition contained a pair of *Lives* and a comparison, but some of the latter are lost), that is, not quite half-way through the whole set of 23. Besides the full-scale *Life of Pericles*, miscellaneous information about that statesman is contained in the *Lives* of Cimon, Nicias and Alcibiades. There is also some relevant material scattered though the moral writings.

2. THE WRITING OF BIOGRAPHY BEFORE PLUTARCH

Although it is difficult to get a clear grasp of the *genre* of biography before Plutarch, it is important to try to fill in the picture, however tentatively, in order to reach a just estimate of Plutarch's own achievement.

As early as the fifth century B.C. works were composed which seem to have had a biographical component but they have mostly disappeared and it is not always possible to tell from later references whether they were genuine biographies. In any case they seem not to have had any great impact, nor did they influence schools of writers to take up biography as a literary form. We hear of works 'On Homer' by Stesimbrotus—to whom we shall return—and a certain Theagenes of Rhegium (c. 500 B.C.), but it is not clear whether, if at all, they recorded material about Homer's life, or were mainly interested in explaining his poetry (Theagenes is said to have been 'the first' to write about Homer, and he originated the allegorical interpretation of Homer's gods). Another early-fifth century writer, Skylax of Caryanda, is reported to have written a life of a contemporary historical figure, the tyrant Heracleides of Mylasa.

It has been claimed that the first glimmerings of true biography can be detected in Stesimbrotus of Thasos, whose information about Pericles will be discussed more fully in the next section. As will be seen, Stesimbrotus does seem to have had a genuine interest in personal aspects of his subjects, for example, education and temperament, but on the basis of what remains, his book cannot be put into any definite class or genre. The historians Herodotus and Thucydides both recognized that great historical events are often best explained as resulting from the plans and actions of outstanding (for better or worse) individuals. The section at the end of his first book in which Thucydides pauses to record events in the lives of Pausanias and Themistocles amply attests to the historian's interest in biography. Two short works from the fourth century about contemporary figures, Isocrates' *Evagoras* and Xenophon's *Agesilaus* (both referred to by Plutarch), give idealized portraits of their subjects and were intended primarily to eulogize. The *Evagoras*, however, contains a comparison with Cyrus the Great, and *Agesilaus*, for all its large component of military history (which must have been very much to Xenophon's taste), also gives a catalogue of Agesilaus' virtues, as

6

illustrated by his actions. In some respects, then, both works can be said to be forerunners of Plutarch's biographies.

The first scholars to interest themselves in biography as a subject of research were Aristotle and his successors. Most of this material is now lost but a few titles and in one case a substantial papyrus-fragment survive. The fourth-century Athenian statesman Demetrius of Phaleron, a pupil of Aristotle's colleague and successor, Theophrastus, wrote a monograph on Demosthenes and included biographical material about Aristeides in a work entitled *Apology of Socrates* (see Plutarch, *Life of Aristeides* ch. 27). Those writers who were themselves philosophers appear to have been mainly interested in the earlier 'masters' of philosophy, although some showed a broader biographical interest. Aristotle's pupil Aristoxenus, whose main importance is in the history of music, wrote a work entitled *Lives of Men* whose subjects included Pythagoras, Socrates and Plato; one of Aristoxenus' working assumptions was that actions manifest character. Hermippus of Smyrna (third century B.C.) wrote works on lawgivers, the Seven Wise Men, philosophers, orators, physicians, and probably also poets. Plutarch cites him several times in the *Solon* and *Demosthenes*, and it used to be thought that Plutarch drew on him widely elsewhere, but without acknowledging his debt; the theory cannot be disproved, but it seems intrinsically unlikely. Hermippus seems to have been interested in the personal and not always edifying aspects of his subjects' lives and Duane R. Stuart writes of 'the easy credulity and the appetite for the marvellous' reflected in his biographical writings (*Epochs of Greek and Roman Biography*, p. 164). Another prolific biographer, roughly contemporary with Hermippus, was Satyrus. His collection of *Lives* (*Bioi*) also covered a wide range: kings, philosophers, orators, generals, poets. A substantial section of his *Life of Euripides* was discovered on a papyrus from Oxyrhynchus, which was published in 1912; it threw new but not altogether reassuring light on his methods as a biographer. First, the work is a dialogue, and may have been influenced by the dialogues of Plato and some of his successors. Second, the piece is heavily anecdotal and proceeds from incidents in Euripides' plays to inferences about events in the poet's own life. On the other hand, Satyrus does seem to transmit some new factual material about Euripides and arranges details about his life in a broad chronological scheme.

Antigonus of Carystus, a bronze-worker by training, composed, about 240 B.C., lives of philosophers of his own time or the preceding generation. His work has been described by Momigliano as 'amateurish' and the citations that survive show him rather given to sensationalism and scandal-mongering.

Biography at Rome had its own distinctive roots in the eulogies pronounced at funerals of distinguished Romans, and the composing of prose encomia of great figures of the past was one of the standard training-exercises for the budding orator. The formal genre of biographical writing, however, was generally believed by the Romans themselves to have begun in 39 B.C. with the publication of M. Terentius Varro's *Hebdomades* or *Imagines* in 15 books. A novel feature of the work was that, as well as 700 biographical sketches of famous Greeks and Romans, set side-by-side in some kind of comparative way, it also contained cameo pictures of these individuals; if it contained a 'Pericles', as seems likely, the accompanying picture was probably based on a copy derived from the well-known bust by the Athenian sculptor Cresilas alluded to by the elder Pliny, *Natural Histories* 34.74. Other Roman biographers named in the same company as Varro are a certain Santra, who is mentioned by Suetonius (for whom, see below) and may therefore have been among the latter's sources, and Augustus' Spanish freedman, C. Julius Hyginus, who became head of the Palatine Library and wrote a work with the title *On Famous Men* or *On the Lives and Deeds of Illustrious Men*. Nothing of either of these survives.

Sometime between 32 and 24 B.C. Cornelius Nepos published his *On Illustrious Men*. Nepos is cited several times by Plutarch in the Roman *Lives* and since he conceived his work, too, along comparative lines (various categories of outstanding individuals, with foreigners, mainly Greeks, in the first of a pair of books and their Roman counterparts in the second) it is likely that he exerted an influence on Plutarch. What survives is the book *On outstanding Leaders of Foreign Nations*, but other sections dealt with Kings, Lawgivers, Orators, Poets, Historians, Philosophers and Grammarians. Another work of Nepos which does not survive, but which may have provided Plutarch with material, was a collection of *Examples*, a miscellaneous assortment of remarkable deeds and sayings of famous men (a similar compilation survives by Valerius Maximus, who wrote about 50 years after Nepos).

Roman biography came into its own with C. Suetonius Tranquillus. After holding various posts in the imperial court of Trajan, he was dismissed by Hadrian. Titles of works ascribed to him show that he had a cataloguer's interest in, for example, Greek and Roman festivals, famous courtesans, terms of abuse. His work as a biographer significantly improved from the summary and rather off-hand *Lives of famous Grammarians* to the more detailed and critical *Lives of the Poets*, from which survive lives of Terence, Virgil and Horace, as well as several biographies preserved under his name, but which may not have been written by him. Suetonius' reputation as a biographer, however, rests mainly on his *Lives of the Twelve Caesars*. His approach to biography appears, on first reading, to resemble Plutarch's (both men were working at about the same time but the *Twelve Caesars* was probably published later than Plutarch's *Lives*);

in the case of the emperors Galba and Otho they even shared the same subject—Plutarch published these apparently before conceiving the project of the *Parallel Lives*—although no direct influence can be traced by either writer on the other. The differences between them, however, are more striking than the similarities. Suetonius approaches the character of his chosen subject in a more mechanical way. He selects—almost catalogues—virtues and vices (more frequently the latter) which he then proceeds to illustrate with anecdotes which are pointed and amusing, or, more often, simply lurid or scandalous, but which rarely make any plausible claim to being historically true. Above all, Suetonius never shows Plutarch's high-minded purpose of drawing universal moral lessons from his material; even more than recording facts about the emperors, Suetonius' purpose seems to have been to entertain and even shock his readers.

3. PERICLES IN THE HISTORICAL AND BIOGRAPHICAL TRADITION

As the leading statesman of Athens' 'Golden Age' Pericles was clearly an individual about whom ordinary Greeks and Romans of the first century A.D. would have known something, and the educated classes a good deal. But the biographical material had been filtered through the rhetorical and anecdotal tradition, and so the transmission was (as we shall see) rather selective and intended to illustrate just a few clichés of his personality and abilities. So Plutarch had to do considerable spade-work in the historical sources to produce his full-scale portrait.

Fifth-century sources

Pericles is mentioned only once by Herodotus (6.131), in connection with the dream that his mother Agariste is alleged to have had just before he was born that she would 'give birth to a lion'. It would have been most unusual for Plutarch either not to know the story, or to fail to mention it if he knew it; he does not disappoint (see chap. 3 below). An outline of events in Pericles' later career, most notably the campaign to suppress the rebellion of Samos, was given by Thucydides. The historian also (if we read between his lines) provides a basis for that view of Pericles which made him out to be aloof, if not arrogant, and unwilling to compromise his lofty principles simply to gain the approval of the rabble. Some information of a miscellaneous and anecdotal kind must have been contained in the work entitled Epidēmiai ('Sojourns' or 'Stopovers') by Ion of Chios (c. 490–before 421 B.C.). From Plutarch's citations of this work in the *Life of Cimon*, it is clear that it presented a very flattering picture of this antagonist of Pericles who, in Ion's estimation at any rate, suffered by comparison; the contrast in personal manner between the two men is made explicit in the citation in *Pericles* 5 (see note below).

The earliest that we can detect any special biographical interest in Pericles for his own sake is in the essay by Stesimbrotus of Thasos, *On Themistocles, Thucydides [son of Melesias] and Pericles* published in about 420 B.C. Once again, so far as we can judge from the citations in the *Cimon* and *Pericles*, the latter came off rather the worse by contrast to the (in Stesimbrotus' view, at least) rougher but more genuine and down-to-earth Cimon. It was alleged against Pericles that he reproached Cimon's twin sons by an Arcadian woman because of their mother's foreign origins (*Cim.* 16; cf. *Per.* 29). Stesimbrotus is also named as the source for the gossip that linked Pericles with his son's wife (*Per.* 13, 36) and for the story that Elpinice, Cimon's sister, appealed to Pericles to be lenient at her brother's trial (*Cim.* 14; see note on *Per.* 10 below). It was not all scandal, however, for once Plutarch cites (only to disagree with) Stesimbrotus for a detail in the Samian campaign (chap. 26 below).

Comedy is not history, but what the contemporary political satirists were poking fun at gives us an idea of those personal characteristics or actions of Pericles that made an impression on the ordinary Athenians of his day. We have Plutarch to thank for being inquisitive enough to look into these comic writers (whether directly or through an anthology is a vexed question, to which no definite answer can be given) and intelligent enough to include the information in his *Life*. Besides the specific information dealt with at greater length in the notes on chapters 3, 13 and 24—his elongated head, his liaison with Aspasia and his patronage of Pheidias, 'Olympian' arrogance, and certain items in his domestic and foreign policy (the building program, especially the 'Long Walls' to the Peiraeus and the Odeon; his treatment of the allies; the war with Samos and the Megarian Decree)—a feature of his leadership which must have accounted for a large measure of his popular appeal and was frequently cited in the later rhetorical tradition was his ability to charm and sway an audience. This comes across clearly in some lines of Aristophanes' older contemporary, Eupolis, which are cited several times by later writers (but not, oddly enough, by Plutarch):

> He was the strongest of men at public speaking:
> When he got up to speak, he left behind
> (Like good runners do) the other orators by ten full feet.
> You could say that he was quick, but speed wasn't everything,
> For a kind of persuasiveness settled on his lips
> So that he could cast a spell, and he alone of orators
> Used to leave his sting behind in those who heard him.
> (fr. 98, Edmonds)

(For a more detailed account of these comic fragments see Endnote A, 'Pericles and the Comic Poets.')

For the philosopher Plato, Pericles joins company with other great figures from the fifth century as men who were pragmatically successful politicians but basically without principle. In Plato's eyes, they looked after the Athenians' material well-being—and so assured their own continuing popularity—by providing the city with walls and dockyards, but they failed to bring about any real moral improvement in their 'charges', the citizens whose welfare they had undertaken to protect. Plato was prepared to argue that Pericles, so far from improving the Athenians, left them worse than he had found them; by introducing payment for discharging certain civic responsibilities, Pericles made the Athenians 'lazy, cowards, babblers and money-grubbing' (*Gorgias 515*, where it is also noted that the people themselves turned against him at the end of his career; see chap. 35 below). Pericles is faulted, too, for being unable to teach his sons his own special skill, statesmanship (*Protagoras* 319 and elsewhere; this rather unfair criticism was also made against other politicians like Themistocles). Plato is our oldest source for the story that Pericles owed a debt of gratitude to Anaxagoras for teaching him 'elevation' of thought (*Phaedrus* 270, where the tone is somewhat flippant and disparaging; see chaps. 4 and 8 below, where Plato is specifically mentioned) and a passing reference at *Letters* II.311A—it is uncertain whether or not all these Letters were really written by Plato—shows that the relationship had become a trite commonplace. Pericles' outstanding abilities as a speaker are glanced at (*Symposium* 215) and the topic is given a satirical twist in *Menexenus*: Pericles owed his success at speaking mainly to the expert tutelage of his mistress, Aspasia (235E; compare chap. 24 below). Other names were recorded of men who had 'taught,' or at least exerted a strong influence on, Pericles: Pythocleides (chap. 4 below, where the reference to Aristotle is probably an error); Damon (chap. 4 below), an influential musician mentioned several times by Plato (linked with Pericles at *Alcibiades* I, 118 and Isocrates *Oration* 15, 235); and—if he is indeed to be distinguished from the preceding—Damonides, whose name Plutarch found in Aristotle (*Constitution of the Athenians* 27.4; cf. chap. 9 below).

In his researches into the history of constitutions Aristotle discovered some further facts about Pericles: his involvement with Ephialtes in 'docking' the old court of the Areopagus and transferring some of its jurisdiction to the people's courts (*Const. of the Athenians* 27.1, whose attribution to Aristotle has been questioned; *Politics* 1274a8; cf. chaps. 7 and 9 below) and his law requiring that both parents be Athenians for a child to be a genuine Athenian citizen (*Const.* 26.4). The charge that Pericles introduced pay for public service is substantiated in one particular, his introduction of payment for jury-duty (*Const.* 27.3, *Politics* 1274a8), but his motivation in so doing is given a sinister and self-serving twist: he was attempting to 'out-demagogue' Cimon, whose family wealth put him into a position of offering the Athenians largesse of various kinds (*Const.* 27.3-4, an interpretation taken over by Plutarch; cf. chap. 9 below). Plutarch cites Aristotle twice for supplementary information on the Samian War (chaps. 26 and 28 below), and it has been suggested that this may derive from the *Constitution of the Samians*. The Samians likewise figure in an apophthegm assigned to Pericles in the *Rhetoric*: he allegedly likened them to 'babies who accept the sop, but cry while doing so' (1407a). Twice in the *Rhetoric* Aristotle cites what must have been one of Pericles' most memorable comparisons: the death of young Athenians on military campaign was 'as if spring had been taken out of the year' (1365a11, 1411a1; Herodotus [7.162] ascribed the same metaphor to the Sicilian tyrant Gelon, but with a somewhat different purport).

Other philosophical writers are credited with having transmitted information about Pericles. In an essay included among Plutarch's *Moralia* but probably not written by him, a long excerpt is quoted from an untitled work by Protagoras, the sophist and contemporary of Socrates who took part in the foundation of Thurii (see chap. 11 below). Protagoras is reported to have commented on the stoical way that Pericles bore the deaths of his two sons Xanthippus and Paralos in the Great Plague of 430 B.C. (*Moralia* 118E-F). A certain Aeschines, who was a follower of Socrates and who wrote dialogues named after historical figures, is known to have composed one entitled *Aspasia*. It was probably in this work that Aeschines told the story, which Plutarch records in chap. 32, of how Pericles broke into tears during Aspasia's trial for impiety and begged the jury to acquit her. Aeschines may also be the source of the item in chap. 24, that Pericles never left his house or returned to it without kissing Aspasia. Another follower of Socrates, Antisthenes, who was one of the founders of the 'Cynic' school of philosophy, wrote a work also entitled *Aspasia* about which almost nothing is known beyond the fact that Pericles' sons Xanthippus and Paralus were accused of cohabiting with men who were notorious homosexuals and social outcasts. A later writer also names Antisthenes as the source of a scurrilous story: Pericles exacted sexual favours from Elpinice, Cimon's sister, as the price for bringing about her brother's recall from exile (see chap. 10 below).

Several successors of Aristotle in the so-called 'Peripatetic school', although they did not turn to full-scale biography as did Hermippus and Satyrus, nevertheless recorded information about Pericles in their other works. Aristotle's colleague and successor, Theophrastus, is cited by Plutarch for three details: the ten-talent bribe to Sparta was paid not once but annually (chap. 23); the prosecutor at his trial in 430 B.C. was named Simmias (chap. 35; other sources supplied different names); and during his last illness he disparaged the supposed curative properties of an amulet he had been given (chap. 38). Heracleides of Pontus named Lakratidas as his prosecutor and said that Pericles, after divorcing his wife, squandered most of his wealth on Aspasia. Aristophanes (*Acharn.* 523 ff.) had drawn a ridiculous connection between Aspasia and the so-called 'Megarian Decree', which was popularly thought to have caused the war with Sparta; Clearchus of Soli, writing in the early third century B.C., gave this a sinister twist: Pericles 'threw all Greece into turmoil' because of her. Demetrius of Phaleron criticized the expenditure of such large sums on the Propylaea.

There were conflicting accounts of Pericles' involvement in the trial of Anaxagoras. Besides that given by Plutarch in chap. 32, that Pericles 'was so alarmed for Anaxagoras' safety that he smuggled him out of the city', Hieronymus of Rhodes, writing in the mid-third century, reported that Pericles brought his old mentor into the courtroom in such a wasted condition that the jurors acquitted him out of pity (see chap. 16 below for traces of the tradition that Anaxagoras physically neglected himself). Roughly contemporary with Hieronymus was Hermippus, whose work as a professional biographer has already been mentioned. His version was somewhat more rhetorical: Pericles argued before the assembly that since the people had no fault to find with his management of the city's affairs, they should cease their anger against his old teacher; Anaxagoras was released but committed suicide out of humiliation. Sotion, who wrote a *Succession of Philosophers* about 175 B.C., held the view that in spite of Pericles' defense, Anaxagoras was fined five talents and banished from Athens (this is in fact the likeliest account). In chap. 7 below and elsewhere, Plutarch quotes a witticism by the late Peripatetic Critolaus (c. 150 B.C.), who compared Pericles to the official state galleys *Salaminia* and *Paralos*: he only appeared in public on special occasions.

Orators

The fourth-century orators, whose interest in earlier Athenian history was somewhat superficial and who tend to re-use a selected number of stock examples (usually by way of contrast with contemporary politicians or trends), singled out only a few of Pericles' qualities and achievements. Isocrates praised him for wisdom and moderation, for his successful prosecution of the war with Samos, for the magnificent buildings on the Acropolis (the theme is a commonplace deriving from Thucydides' Funeral Speech, and finds its way with embellishments into chaps. 12 and 13 below). He notes Pericles' instruction by Anaxagoras and Damon and his own tutelage of

13

Alcibiades. Isocrates eulogizes Pericles for having 'left his family property less than he had inherited it from his father'. (This item is taken over by Plutarch at the end of chap. 15 and it may rest on no more solid evidence than Thucydides' report [2.13] that Pericles turned over his country estates to be public property, to forestall any odium if the Spartans should leave them unravaged.) Isocrates also approves of the fact that Pericles 'filled the Acropolis with silver and gold, and made private homes full of great prosperity and wealth', the very thing that Plato objected to since, in his opinion, this increased national prosperity made the ordinary Athenian lazy and soft.

Later historians

The first man to write a History of Attica, or *Atthis*, was Hellanicus of Lesbos, whose work was published in time for Thucydides to censure it for chronological inexactitude (I.97). We also learn from Thucydides that Hellanicus treated the period between the Persian and Peloponnesian Wars. Not one of the half-dozen or so citations from his work preserved in later authors that touch on events or persons in the fifth century is even remotely connected with Pericles, and any argument that details in late accounts which conflict with Thucydides' version of events in this period derive ultimately from Hellanicus is just so much conjecture. All writers of *Atthides* who followed Hellanicus must have had something to say about Pericles, if only to mention his contributions to the growth of Athens' power and his involvement in the events which led up to the war with Sparta. Androtion, a pupil of Isocrates and an important political figure in his own right, is thought to have published his *Atthis* about 340 B.C. Although this theory has had its opponents, it has generally been maintained that Androtion gave his work a 'conservative' slant. Fragments of his survive that touch on the ostracism of Thucydides, son of Melesias (see chaps. 6, 14 and 16 below), the campaign against Samos, for which Androtion provides the names of the other nine generals who were Pericles' colleagues in the first year (441/0 B.C.), and the first Peloponnesian invasion of Attica in 431 B.C. Phanodemus is cited twice by Plutarch in his *Life of Cimon* for biographical details, but nothing remains of any episode with which Pericles was directly connected. Philochorus, the last and most scholarly of the Atthidographers, composed his work in the opening decades of the third century. More remains of his treatment of events in the fifth century than of that by the other writers on Athenian history. He dealt with Ephialtes' reforms of the Areopagus in 462/1 B.C. (again, Pericles is not mentioned) and the so-called 'Sacred War' for possession of the Delphic shrine in 448; he did mention Pericles' name in connection with the suppression of the revolt of Euboea in 446/5, and the ostracism of Thucydides son of Melesias a year or so later. He discussed and gave a date for the beginning of the Propylaea (437/6 B.C.) and quite a full citation survives of his account of charges laid against Pheidias in connection with the gold and ivory statue of Athena Parthenos which he sculpted 'under the supervision of Pericles'. Philochorus' account, besides giving a date to the episode which some scholars find impossibly early (438/7 B.C.), differs in several important respects from that given by Plutarch in chap. 31 below. According to Philochorus, who dates these events to the archon-year in which Pheidias' statue of Athena was completed, the sculptor was charged with fraud in his accounting for the ivory used and, to avoid prosecution or possibly after sentence was passed, went to Elis where he started work on his famous seated Zeus at Olympia (which Plutarch mentions in chap. 2 below). Philochorus also reported, probably on the basis of the official records, that Pericles was in charge of building the gymnasium in the area known as the Lyceum, near where Aristotle later established his philosophical school.

Ephorus of Cyme in Asia Minor wrote a *Universal History* which covered events from the Trojan War down to his own time in the 330's. In addition to the citations specifically from this work, several of which touch on episodes in Pericles' career, it is generally held that he was the major source used by Diodorus of Sicily for events in mainland Greece; Diodorus lived and wrote in the time of Augustus, and his narrative of the fifth century survives virtually entire. In fact, Diodorus specifically cites Ephorus for his account of events leading up to the outbreak of the war with Sparta, and it is this which Plutarch seems to have relied heavily upon in chaps. 30 and following. In Ephorus' view (which may be based on nothing more than a too-literal interpretation of some far-fetched jokes in Aristophanes), Pericles used the war as a smokescreen to distract public attention from his own personal involvement with Pheidias and Anaxagoras, who had in turn come under fire as a means of indirect attack upon Pericles himself. This fantastic reconstruction should be considered highly suspect not only because of the sordid motives it ascribes to ˏ ᴄ ricles but because it glosses over complex questions of chronology in the trials of Pheidias and Anaxagoras. Ephorus is cited by Plutarch twice in his narrative of the Samian War (chaps. 27 and 28 below). With Euboea and Megara both in revolt from Athens in 446/5, and a Spartan army not only having crossed the borders but having advanced as far as Eleusis and the Thriasian plain, it was a particularly tense time for Pericles. The Spartan army withdrew, thus leaving Pericles a free hand to put down the revolt. The Spartan king was exiled and his adviser condemned to death, allegedly for having taken a bribe. Thucydides alludes to the story but gives no details; common gossip (as early as Aristophanes, *Clouds* 859 but fully

15

developed in chaps. 22-23 below) had it that it was Pericles who had used ten talents of public money to bribe the Spartans. Ephorus (if he is quoted correctly by the anonymous source) gave the figure as twenty talents, and added that the Spartan king was fined 15 talents for his part in the affair.

Theopompus of Chios, a contemporary of Ephorus, wrote a *History of Philip of Macedon* in 58 books of which the tenth contained a long and celebrated digression on Athenian demagogues. Although the treatment of Pericles must have been fairly extensive, all that survives is a reference to his opponent Thucydides' father's name, and to the recall of Cimon after only five years, not the usual ten, of his ostracism had elapsed; in chap. 10 Plutarch reports that 'some' authorities said Pericles himself moved the decree of recall and it is probable (even if not quite certain) that Theopompus was among them. Idomeneus of Lampsacus (c. 300 B.C.) also wrote a work *On Demagogues* and it is probably from this work that Plutarch quotes (but only to reject) the story that Pericles secretly engineered the murder of his erstwhile associate, Ephialtes, 'out of envy for his reputation' (chap. 10 below; in chap. 35 Idomeneus is cited for the name of Pericles' prosecutor in 430). Plutarch is no more trusting of the Samian writer Duris, whose *Annals of Samos* included an account of the barbarities allegedly perpetrated by Pericles against his defeated opponents in the Samian War; as Plutarch himself notes, Duris tended to 'dramatize' events and was in any case, as a Samian, hardly likely to be objective in his reporting (chap. 28). The imputation of a personal and dishonorable motive for starting the war, that Pericles did it just to gratify Aspasia (chaps. 24 and 25), is also due to Duris (Jacoby 76 F 65).

Pericles at Rome

What was the 'standard' picture of Pericles in the late Republic, and to what sources would an educated Roman of the period have gone for information about the Greek statesman? Among Varro's seven hundred *Imagines*, already mentioned, there would certainly have been one devoted to Pericles, but whether he found a place in the biographical writings of Hyginus and Santra is unknown, since nothing of their work survives. Cicero's dialogue *Brutus*, composed in 46 B.C., was in effect a history of oratory up to Cicero's time, and so Pericles' accomplishments as a speaker are naturally given special prominence. In fact, several of the items concerning Pericles recur in the two 'companion' works *The Orator* and *On Oratory*: his debt to Anaxagoras for mental discipline and elevation of thought is alluded to no less than five times, and in one place Cicero specifically refers to his source, Plato's Phaedrus. Cicero also mentions more than once Eupolis' lines, already quoted, about the lasting impression Pericles' oratory made on his audiences. Some of this material recurs in Plutarch's *Life*: Pericles' rather stern and unjovial manner (chap. 5); his quip to Sophocles about a general's obligations to keep his mind as well as his hands clean (chap. 8); his reliance on the scientific theories of Anaxagoras to quell popular superstition at the time of an eclipse (chap. 35, with chap. 6); the allegation that Pheidias included a self-portrait on the shield of Athena Parthenos 'since he was not allowed to inscribe his name' (chap. 31); the well-known passage from Aristophanes' *Acharnians* ridiculing Pericles' 'Olympian' punishment of the Megarians (chap. 30). Cicero twice refers to 'writings' by Pericles, where Plutarch in chap. 8 says specifically that he 'left nothing behind him in writing except for the decrees he proposed' (we learn from Quintilian that there was a dispute about the authenticity of speeches passing under Pericles' name). And Cicero is our only witness to Demetrius of Phaleron's attacks against Pericles for the high cost of the Propylaea.

Scholars believe that the book of Nepos' *Lives* in which he treated 'Generals of Foreign Nations' survives complete; if so, it is hard to understand why Pericles was omitted. (It has been suggested that Pericles, as well as other famous Athenians like Solon and Nicias, may have been included in a category other than 'generals'.) In any case, some information about Pericles would have been recorded in another of Nepos' works, *Chronicles* (*Chronica*), a compendium of world history in three books, which probably proceeded chronologically. As noted in Sect. 2, Nepos' book of *Examples* was a forerunner of Valerius Maximus' *Memorable Deeds and Sayings*, which was dedicated to Tiberius and probably published shortly after 31 A.D. It is our only surviving example of a type of handbook intended for use by public speakers, along the lines of contemporary books of 'Jokes for all Occasions'. It has been called 'shallow, sententious and bombastic'. Some of the anecdotes already gleaned from Cicero recur in Valerius' miscellany: Pericles' use of astronomical information acquired from Anaxagoras to reassure the citizens who were fearful over an eclipse; the rebuke to Sophocles for eyeing a handsome youth; his honeyed oratory, even when proposing a politically unpalatable course. Valerius relates an anecdote concerning a piece of worldly wisdom given by Alcibiades. When Pericles was worrying about how to render his accounts, his kinsman and ward advised him to consider rather how *not* to render them. This story Plutarch uses in the *Life of Alcibiades* and it occurs again in *Sayings of Kings and Commanders*, a collection similar to Valerius', for which Plutarchan authorship has (probably wrongly) been claimed. Its first recorded occurrence, in Diodorus, where it serves as a lead-in to the gossip that the war was nothing but a smokescreen, has suggested that its ultimate source may be Ephorus. Valerius reports several items not encountered before. As a special honour to Pericles the Athenians Areopagus introduced the custom of granting outstanding citizens the right to wear an olive wreath, and even after losing two excellent (!) sons to the plague he kept his head crowned, 'so that no domestic wound would detract from the ancient rite'; it was such strength of character that earned for him the title 'Olympian'. Valerius records an interesting and instructive anecdote linking Pericles and the tyrant Peisistratus. An old man who when young had heard Peisistratus speak remarked, on hearing the first speech by the youthful Pericles, that the two men's oratorical styles were so similar that the Athenians should beware a deeper similarity between them. The story with some modifications is retailed by Plutarch in chap. 7 below and he records elsewhere (*Mor.* 795C-D) an analogous anecdote linking Pericles and Demosthenes. Similarity of oratorical styles betokening similarity of political attitude was, or was on its way to becoming, a cliché. Valerius misremembers a point in Aristophanes' *Frogs*, for he attributes to a resurrected Pericles the advice to treat the highspirited Alcibiades with utmost care, as if he were some proud but possibly dangerous lion, whereas in the play of Aristophanes it is Aeschylus who gives this advice (possibly there is some confusion with Eupolis' *Demes* where the dead Pericles, among others, was brought back to life to advise his countrymen at a critical time in the war).

The Elder Pliny, in his *Natural Histories*, which were still unfinished at his death in A.D. 79, makes several references to Pericles. He tells the story, found in chap. 13 below, of Pericles' dream and miraculous cure of the workman who had fallen from the roof of the Parthenon (in a variation on this anecdote, Pericles addresses a comment to a slave who has fallen from the roof of a house or an olive-tree [Hieronymus of Rhodes 19 Wehrli; Diogenes Laertius 9.82]). It is unknown on whose authority Pliny credited Pericles (or the Samians!—the source for this confusion may be that they were first used in the Samian revolt) with having invented the type of ship known as a 'cavalry transport', as well as the grappling-irons or 'claws' used in boarding operations during naval engagements. Pliny mentions a well-known portrait-bust by Cresilas (it is doubtless to copies of this that Plutarch alludes in chap. 3) as well as an otherwise unrecorded picture by the fourth-century painter Aristolaus.

In about 95 A.D. the rhetorician Quintilian published his Education of the Orator (Institutio Oratoria) and in it several of the commonplaces concerning Pericles reappear: the uplifting influence of Anaxagoras, Pericles' calming the people's fears after an eclipse. Quintilian notes that the comic writers adverted to the 'thunder and lightning' of his delivery, but several times insists that judgements of him as an orator cannot rest on any genuine speeches; and he alludes in more than one place to Eupolis' celebrated lines, already quoted. Quintilian also preserves the anecdote recounted by Plutarch in chap. 8 below and elsewhere that whenever Pericles 'rose to speak, he uttered a prayer that no word might escape his lips which was unsuited to the matter in hand.'

4. PLUTARCH'S METHODS

As can readily be seen from the foregoing survey, the material available to Plutarch when he set out to write his *Life of Pericles* was fairly extensive, but of a very mixed order. To say that he is 'only as good as his sources' is an oversimplification but, as with most such, there is a certain degree of truth in it. He names some 22 different authors in the work, several not for matters of substance concerning Pericles. It does much to inspire confidence in the basic soundness of his approach that he cites Thucydides by name six times (in chaps. 9, 15, 16, 28 twice, and 33) and it is clear that elsewhere, too, Plutarch is drawing mainly on Thucydides' narrative without naming the historian directly. He takes the detail in chap. 3 about Agariste's dream, as we have seen, from Herodotus. Plutarch cites other contemporary or near-contemporary testimony, but he does not take over their opinions uncritically. He seems to recognize Ion's bias in favour of Cimon (and so against Pericles): 'we need not pay much attention to Ion . . .' (chap. 5). Stesimbrotus' charge that Pericles had seduced his son's wife is labelled by Plutarch not only 'shocking' but 'completely unfounded' (chap. 13; cf. chap. 36). The citations in chaps. 27 and 28 show that Plutarch had consulted (or remembered) Ephorus on the siege of Samos, but the historian's testimony regarding Artemon 'the Carried-around' (*Periphoretus*) is tested against that of Heracleides Ponticus. And Plutarch can hardly conceal his disdain of the Samian Duris' exaggerations: he 'magnifies these events (i.e. Pericles' vindictive punishment of the Samians) into a tragedy'; he 'is apt to overstep the limits of the truth,' Plutarch comments shrewdly, 'even when there are no personal interests of his at stake' (chap. 28). Plutarch scornfully dismisses Idomeneus' scurrilous report that Pericles engineered the assassination of Ephialtes (chap. 10).

To balance a healthy skepticism in the 'official' historical record, Plutarch shows the good judgement to draw abundantly upon comic writers—whether he knew their works directly or only through anthologies and compendia has been a subject of interminable debate—whose testimony, since it reveals the preoccupations of ordinary Athenians, is of incalculable value. Thus, he cites by name Aristophanes (chaps. 26 and 30 and probably also without naming him in chap. 32), Cratinus (chaps. 3, 13 and 24), Eupolis (chaps. 3 and 24), Hermippus (chap. 33), Plato the Comedian (chap. 4) and Telecleides (chaps. 3 and 16), as well as certain comic writers who are not named (chaps. 8 and 16). As Gomme remarks, it is to Plutarch's great credit that 'he preserves something of what Thucydides purposely omitted, the biographical detail, the political lampoons, the mockery of the comic poets' (*Historical Commentary on Thucydides*, vol. I, p. 74). In addition, according to Holden, 'he has furnished us with details not to be found elsewhere, and the anecdotes, even the scandalous gossip, which he reports, give us a glimpse of the world in which Pericles moved' (Plutarch's *Life of Pericles*, Intro. p. xxx). And it is to Plutarch's great credit that he seems to have been the first (so far as we can tell) to have undertaken a full-scale biography of Pericles.

Few modern scholars any longer believe that Plutarch lifted his material whole from a predecessor (in the past, a favourite candidate had been the Peripatetic biographer, Hermippus [see above, sec. 2]), and without acknowledging the debt. On the other hand, to say that Plutarch did his own 'research' into the sources may be misleading; Plutarch reads, records, excerpts or remembers; the result is partly derivative, partly his own, and quite often unsystematic. As Gomme put it: 'He selects from a mass of material, as he says more than once . . ., and arranges it himself' (*Commentary*, p. 82). At the beginning of the *Life of Demosthenes* (a passage often cited in this connection) Plutarch talks of the necessity a writer on a historical topic feels to reside in a famous and populous city like Athens or Rome, where 'he may . . . have access to all kinds of books'. Then Plutarch makes a noteworthy addition: 'through hearsay and personal inquiry he may succeed in uncovering facts which often escape the chroniclers and are preserved in more reliable form in human memory' (*Demosthenes* chap. 2, trans. Scott-Kilvert). Elsewhere he insists that he has 'tried to collect with care' facts which, he says, 'have eluded most writers altogether, or have been mentioned only haphazardly by others, or are recorded only in decrees or in ancient votive inscriptions' (*Life of Nicias*, chap. 1, trans. Scott-Kilvert). Research in books, and personal investigation among the surviving records and archaeological monuments: perfectly respectable methods of enquiry, the second favoured by no less venerable a forerunner than Herodotus. To these must be added a 'source' of lesser value, the stories 'told in the schools of philosophy' (chap. 35 below).

We hear, too, of collections of notes (*hypomnēmata*) which Plutarch says he made (*Moralia* 457 D, 464 F). These would have been similar to the 'apophthegms' or collections of sayings of famous men, which form a separate part of the Moralia as these have come down to us, although it is exceedingly doubtful that these were written by Plutarch; two of the four *bons mots* attributed to Pericles there (*Mor.* 186 C-D) recur in the *Life* at chaps. 8 and 28. Apart from the notes he must have taken when he had occasion to use the libraries in the 'great cities', it is quite clear that Plutarch would not have achieved the quantity and variety which his writings manifest without vast industry and, as already remarked, exceptional powers of memory. He allows himself a comment in chap. 24 below that could easily have stood at many other places in his works: 'These details concerning Aspasia come into my mind as I write, and it would have been unnatural to omit them.' This prompted Gomme to comment, 'We must think of him as *in the main* writing from memory, often doubtless from a memory recently refreshed' (*Commentary* I.84). D.A. Russell sums up Plutarch's method as follows: 'Intrinsic probability, external evidence, the known credit of the source all come into his arguments' (*Plutarch*, p. 57).

A.J. Gossage is representative of modern opinion in crediting Plutarch with 'intellectual honesty in reporting what writers before him had written'; it is this basic honesty (which is, however, a subjective judgement and one which cannot be independently verified) that makes it 'probable that he himself had read many, if not most, of the sources that he quotes, and that his biographies were fresh and original in their composition rather than copies or recollections of earlier biographies on the same subjects' (Gossage, 'Plutarch,' p. 52). Barrow goes beyond this to the impression left on us by these Lives as literature: 'Above all [Barrow writes], the singlemindedness and sincerity of the author stand out; with an earnestness which is free from priggishness and a fervour which does not preach he identifies himself with his heroes and does his best to let us see them as human beings, with human strengths and weaknesses' (*Plutarch and his Times* p. 60).

Still, it would be doing Plutarch a disservice to treat his works as primarily exercises in historical research. His chief purpose, as he himself tells us more than once, was moral and ethical, the holding up of great men and their achievements as examples for his readers to admire and also, if possible, to emulate. This ethical purpose also accounts in large part for Plutarch's decision to compare individuals from Greek and Roman history (Varro had earlier paired his subjects in this way, but it is unknown whether this influenced Plutarch). Occasionally men are joined mainly because they had similar careers (e.g. Demosthenes and Cicero), but more often Plutarch matches individuals who seem to him to manifest the same virtues in their lives, as with Pericles and Fabius (see note on end of chap. 2, below). The ethical characteristics which Plutarch particularly wants to analyze are thus thrown into higher relief. Wallace-Hadrill, whose main concern is with Suetonius, stops to remark that Plutarch 'writes as an essayist treating a man's life as a story worth telling for the interest of the tale, and worth discussing for the improvement to be derived from its morals' (*Suetonius*, p. 69). The philosophical (or, perhaps better, psychological) assumption behind Plutarch's avowed purpose he states in chap. 2 below: 'virtue in action immediately takes such hold of a man that he no sooner admires a deed than he sets out to follow in the steps of the doer.' For those mainly interested in Plutarch's subjects as historical figures this approach has its shortcomings. As Russell observes, 'he barely notices the wider historical influence of his heroes, because his eyes are occupied with their individual human qualities' (*Plutarch*, p. 103). 'He is intelligent, but not a scholar,' writes Gossage; 'he is a moralist and an artist' (*ibid.*, p. 66). It is just this informed and honest, but unpedantic, approach, combined with a manifest humanity and a cultivated, wide-ranging taste, and the ability to write in a lively and interesting way, that have made Plutarch a writer who has exerted great influence in later periods of European literature. As Gossage well remarks, 'His philanthropic outlook, his moderation, his variety of interests, his leisurely manner of writing, have had a wide civilizing influence on subsequent ages' (*ibid.*, 66-67).

5. THE STRUCTURE OF 'PERICLES'

Gomme called the *Life of Pericles* 'the most complex and most interesting' of the fifth-century Greek Lives (*Commentary* I. p. 65). The *Life* can be divided into the following main sections (based principally on Gomme; compare also Perrin [1910] 59 ff., Holden xliiff.):

Section I. Chaps. 1-2, Introduction: a somewhat lengthy exposition of what Plutarch perceives as the value of studying the actions of great men.

Section II. Chaps. 3-8, antecedents of Pericles' political career and his personal characteristics, his birth and physical appearance, (3), and (4) his education, especially at the hands of Damon and Anaxagoras; this had an effect upon his manner (5), which was variously considered 'lofty' or 'haughty and disdainful', according to whether one was favourably disposed to him or not. In chap. 6 Plutarch allows himself to ramble somewhat into a disquisition on a topic that was clearly important to him, the value of scientific knowledge in overcoming superstition. In chap. 7 Plutarch attempts to harmonize the undeniable fact of Pericles' immense popular appeal—he was a 'demagogue' in the least offensive sense of that term—and the reputation he had to the end of his life of remaining private and aloof from the common rabble. Plutarch's solution, which may be largely of his own devising (although he seems to have found hints in the Atthis via the Aristotelian *Constitution of Athens* as well as Theopompus), is that Pericles went against his own natural inclinations and Anaxagoras' training in a conscious effort to rival Cimon in the people's affections; consorting with the commons he left to subordinates like Ephialtes. Chap. 8 is a miscellany in which

Plutarch develops the topic of Pericles' skill as a speaker and adds an assortment of anecdoctal material.

Section III. Chaps. 9-14: Pericles' struggles against the most formidable rivals of his early and middle political years, who were, respectively, Cimon and Thucydides, son of Melesias; with the ostracism of the latter in 444/3 B.C., Pericles can relax into the role to which he was best suited by nature and for which his training had equipped him, that of enlightened and benevolent statesman. Note that there was no obvious difference or change in the concrete measures proposed by Pericles at the different stages of his career, although this is not brought out explicitly by Plutarch who may, in fact, have been unaware of it, since in matters of chronology he was what Gomme termed 'carefree'. The difference lies entirely in the sphere of motive: early popular measures like jury-pay (9) and, later, cleruchies (11, with a brief mention at 9), are 'demagogic' while the building-program is 'statesmanly'. Plutarch closes with an extended, factually detailed and almost rhapsodic section on the buildings (end of 12-14) before proceeding to:

Section IV, chaps. 15-37: Pericles' public policy. Even in this last section, which is Thucydidean in inspiration and content, Plutarch reverts to themes he has already introduced: Pericles' quasi-tyrannical rule, which the comedians lampooned; relations with Anaxagoras; his 'loftiness' and 'grandeur' (end of chap. 17). From chaps. 17 on Plutarch narrates those military campaigns and other expeditions that preceded the attack on Samos; the events are only very generally in sequential order, and no firm chronological inferences can be drawn from the narrative. We hear of the notorious and disputed 'Congress Decree' (17; see notes there), his opposition to Tolmides' Boeotian undertaking (18); his expedition to the Chersonese which took place sometime between 449 and 447 B.C., and his campaigns in the Corinthian Gulf and northwest Greece of about 453 (19); his pacifying operations in the Black Sea and settlement at Sinope c. 437 and an allusion to his non- involvement in Egypt of many years earlier (20); the so-called 'Sacred War' in about 448 (21) and the revolts of Euboea and Megara (22 and 23). Chaps. 24 to 28 give an extended account of the suppression of the revolt of Samos, in which Thucydides' own relatively full narrative is supplemented with valuable material from the comedians and later writers hostile to Pericles. In chaps. 29 to 38 Plutarch follows the same procedure in narrating the preliminaries and early years of the war with Sparta: Thucydides provides the basis, but much is added not only from gossip and political satire but also (apparently) from independent sources, some of them probably deriving from primary documents such as the decrees lodged against Pheidias (31), Aspasia (32) and Pericles himself (32 and 35). The *Life* closes with a moving tribute (39); Plutarch is unable to resist returning for one final time to a meditation on the nickname 'Olympian' and a defense of the charge that Pericles' unique and for the most part unchallenged position of power over his fellow-Athenians was little better than a tyranny.

Bibliographical Note

There are two very good books in English about Plutarch: R.H. Barrow, *Plutarch and his Times* (London, Chatto, 1967), and D.A. Russell, *Plutarch* (London, Duckworth, 1973). Students of the *Pericles* will find particularly helpful: Barrow chap. 7, 'The Lives', and Chap. 11, mainly on Plutarch's sources in the *Lives*; Russell chap. 3, 'The Scholar and his Books' and chap. 6, 'An Introduction to the "Lives" '.

Somewhat more specialized is A. Wardman, *Plutarch's Lives* (London, Elek, 1974). There is a brief but informative essay by A.J. Gossage, 'Plutarch', in *Latin Biography*, ed. T.A. Dorey (London, Routledge, 1967), ch. 3, pp. 45-77. See also a comprehensive essay by C.P. Jones, 'Plutarch,' in T.J. Luce, ed., *Ancient Writers, Greece and Rome* (New York: Charles Scribner's sons, 1982) vol. II, pp. 961-983. For the Roman background, especially Nepos, see Edna M. Jenkinson, 'Nepos—an Introduction to Latin Biography' in Dorey, ed., *Latin Biography* (above), pp. 1-15. Somewhat more detailed is Joseph Geiger, *Cornelius Nepos and ancient political Biography* (*Historia Einzelschriften* 47, Stuttgart, 1985).

An absolutely indispensable starting-point for a study of Plutarch's method of composition, especially in the *Pericles*, is A.W. Gomme, *A Historical Commentary on Thucydides*, vol. I (Oxford: Clarendon Press, 1959) pp. 65ff. There is a detailed and very informative analysis of the *Alcibiades* (in some ways quite close to the *Pericles*) in Russell, chap. 7 (adapted from *Proceedings of the Cambridge Philological Society* no. 192 [1966] 37ff.). See also P.A. Stadter, *Plutarch's Historical Methods: an analysis of the 'Mulierum Virtutes'* (Cambridge, Mass., 1965) ch. IV, 'Plutarch's Interest in History', pp. 125-40; A.E. Wardman, 'Plutarch's Methods in the *Lives*', *Classical Quarterly* 21 (1971) 254-61.

The best general introduction to the topic of biographical writing in antiquity is A. Momigliano, *The Development of Greek Biography* (Cambridge, Mass., Harvard, 1971), supplemented by Momigliano's important and somewhat misleadingly-titled article, 'Second Thoughts on Greek Biography' (Mededelingen der koninklijke Nederlandse Akademie van Wetenschappen, afd. Letterkunde, nieuwe reeks, deel 34, no. 7 [Amsterdam], 1971). An older but still very serviceable account is D.R. Stuart, *Epochs of Greek and Roman Biography* (Berkeley, Univ. of California, 1928). A full-length study of Plutarch's contemporary and fellow-biographer has been published by A. Wallace-Hadrill, *Suetonius* (London, Duckworth, 1983).

More detailed analyses of the *Pericles* in English are B. Perrin *Plutarch's 'Cimon' and 'Pericles'* (New York, Scribner's, 1910; Perrin's translation is reprinted in the Loeb Classical Library, *Plutarch's Lives*) and H.A. Holden, *Plutarch's Life of Pericles* (London, Macmillan, 1894; reprinted Chicago, 1983); although Holden's is essentially a commentary on the Greek text, there is much useful material in the Introduction. There is a French translation with brief notes by R. Flacelière and E. Chambry, *Plutarque: Vies*, tome III (Paris, 1964). More advanced students may wish to consult Ekkehard Meinhardt, *Perikles bei Plutarch* (dissertation Frankfurt/Main, 1957) who at pp. 69-76 gives a schematic outline of Plutarch's supposed sources chapter-by-chapter in the *Life*.

Pericles has not been well served by modern historians or biographers writing in English. For those who read French there is Marie Delcourt, *Périclès* (Paris, 1939); I particularly liked chaps. 4, 6 and 10. *Pericles the Athenian* by Rex Warner (Boston and Toronto, 1963) is an intriguing attempt to re-tell the story in the form of fictionalized memoirs by Anaxagoras. Those interested in the history of the period would do well to read Thucydides' *The Peloponnesian War* in Warner's lively and accurate translation (revised ed., Harmondsworth, 1972). A.R. Burn's *Pericles and Athens* (London, 1948) is brief but comprehensive. Recently the University of British Columbia Press has published Malcolm F. McGregor's general study, *The Athenians and their Empire* (Vancouver, 1987).

Note

Occasionally in the *Commentary* below, references occur to 'Fornara' with a section (not page) number. This is a useful collection of translated inscriptions, papyrus documents and other hard-to-find sources: Charles W. Fornara, *Archaic Times to the end of the Peloponnesian War* (2nd ed., Cambridge and New York, 1983).

The Family of Pericles

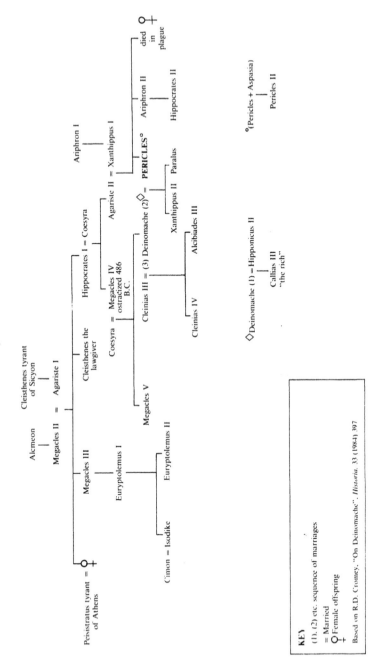

KEY

(1), (2) etc. sequence of marriages

= Married

⚲ Female offspring

Based on R.D. Cromey, "On Deinomache", *Historia* 33 (1984) 397

Commentary

Chaps. 1 and 2 form an Introduction to a series of *Lives* ('Book 10' in Plutarch's own numeration), which appear to have a more overtly ethical purpose than the earlier ones. It is also in Plutarch's manner occasionally to introduce a pair of *Lives* in more general terms, often by touching on points of comparison between his Greek and Roman subjects, before settling into the biography proper (so *Cimon* and *Lucullus*, *Nicias* and *Crassus*). Here he attempts to rationalize his feeling that the study of noble deeds is of a morally more worthy order than the contemplation of, say, works of literature or the visual arts.

Chapter 1

The **emperor Augustus'** rebuke of misplaced affection shown to pet animals is not recorded elsewhere, but the same story is told of a different monarch by Athenaeus (518 F).

In Plutarch's opinion, the morally uplifting material should be presented in a pleasurable way (**models which can inspire . . . through the sense of delight they arouse**) for, as C.P. Jones puts it in discussing this aspect of Plutarch's craft, 'amusement made instruction easier to absorb'. This is, in effect, coating the bitter pill or, in the language of Lucretius, putting honey around the rim of the cup containing unpleasant medicine (*On the Nature of the Universe*, I.936ff.). Plutarch makes this point about the medium being just as important as the message several times in his other works.

Antisthenes was a fourth-century 'Cynic' philosopher, a follower of Socrates, whom Plutarch cites many times; he is known to have written a work entitled *Aspasia* (see above, Intro. sec. 3). **Ismenius** of Thebes in Boeotia was a well known musician on the *aulos* (similar to an oboe) who was also reputed to be rather ostentatious. Underlying the anecdote here is a controversy which seems to have originated in philosophical circles before the end of the fifth century over the value of a musical training (a term which also covered literature and the fine arts) in the formation of generals and politicians. Echoes of this debate can be heard in anecdotes recorded by Plutarch concerning Themistocles and Cimon. It appears that by the end of the fifth century it was 'not done' for gentlemen to show too much expertise in playing instruments, expecially the *aulos* (there was good mythical precedent for the kithara or harp, which Homer says Achilles could play), and it was even possible to cite certain myths involving the goddess Athena to back up this prejudice (compare the story told at length concerning Alcibiades in *Life of Alcibiades*, chap. 2).

The anecdote at the end of the chapter, with Philip rebuking Alexander with **playing the harp . . . as well as that**, illustrates Philip's philistinism as well as Plutarch's acceptance of a hierarchy of skills, with the arts ranking low in the scale; the second element (but not the first) is illustrated by a story told in the *Sayings of Kings and Commanders* (see Intro. above, sec. 3) of an exchange between Philip and a professional harpist. When Philip showed himself willing and able to discuss certain fine points of technique, the musician was horrified; 'May you never fall so low,' he exclaimed, 'as to be better informed in these matters than I.'

Along this same vein, Plutarch devotes a short essay to a defense of the paradoxical position that Athens' true glory rests not on the writings of her historians and dramatists but on the deeds of her statesmen and politicians (*On the Glory of Athens*, *Moralia* 345C-351B).

Plutarch takes up the theme of Pericles' musical education in chap. 4.

Chapter 2

Plutarch is attempting to justify his personal preference (and it is no more than that) for factual accounts of noble deeds (**virtue in action**) over contemplation of works of art or reading poetry. The drift of his argument is not easy to follow and it is in any case based on an inherent ambiguity in the Greek word *kalon*, an ambiguity also present, but to a lesser degree, in the English word 'good'. We use certain terms like 'good', 'noble' to show our approval and commendation of objects which are (aesthetically) beautiful, as well as actions which are (morally) praiseworthy. What is the difference, and is one class to be graded higher than the other? Plutarch's answer — and many may agree with him — is that moral good is of a higher order than aesthetic, but the argument he uses is fallacious, since it introduces a distinction of pragmatic usefulness which will not stand up to close examination.

Works of art, Plutarch argues, **do not arouse the spirit of emulation or create any passionate desire to imitate them** — perhaps not in Plutarch, or men of his temperament, but what of the next man or woman? Any number of noted musicians who lived after J.S. Bach are reported as having been 'inspired' to try to equal or surpass his achievement, and even listeners today claim to be 'inspired' and 'uplifted' by it or other works of art (and Plutarch's near-rhapsody over the Periclean buildings shows that he was not impervious to aesthetic beauty; see chap. 13 below, **makes Pericles' works an object of wonder to us** and following).

In commending **moral good** as having **a power to attract towards itself**, Plutarch does not succeed in distinguishing it from aesthetic beauty; he is simply stating a subjective preference (although many perhaps would agree with him). In classing the activities of artists as **servile tasks** he betrays the same bias as was revealed in chap. 1. Furthermore, there are moral philosophers who whould dispute the distinction he attempts to draw between **imitation** and **understanding of virtuous deeds**; Aristotle for one would have argued that we become good by repeatedly performing good actions, and he believed that the best place to look for role-models was among persons who were genuinely good, whose actions could be imitated. (There is a problem concerning the text at the end of the first paragraph. . . . **does not form . . . by mere imitation** is a translator's interpretation. The Greek has **not . . . by imitation** which, in light of **a keen desire to imitate them** in chap. 1, cannot be what Plutarch intended. C.P. Jones suggests adding a word: **not only by imitation.**)

The artists mentioned by Plutarch at the beginning of the chapter were all outstanding in their respective fields. About **Pheidias** we shall be hearing much more in chaps. 13 and 31-32 below. One of the dates preserved for his removal from Athens was 438/7, after he had completed the Parthenon and its statue of Athena. From there he went to Olympia where he worked on his most famous piece, the seated Zeus mentioned here.

Polycleitus, of Argos or Sicyon, was a sculptor active in the last part of the fifth century. He is praised by Cicero and Pliny the Elder for having captured the perfection of human form, especially in his *Doryphoros* (Spear-carrier) and *Diadoumenos* (Athlete binding his head with a ribbon); he was also noted for the seated statue of Hera for her shrine at Argos, mentioned here.

Anacreon was a writer of love-poetry who worked principally at Samos in the 520's and then in Athens for several decades thereafter.

Philetas of Cos was a writer of elegy who flourished about 300 B.C. and is praised by a later poet as 'versed in all the terms of love and in all its speech'. (It is possible that Plutarch's text originally mentioned Philemon, a long-lived and celebrated comic poet of the late third, early second century B.C.).

Archilochus is rightly considered the first Greek lyric poet, who put much of his own emotions and personality into his work. He was active between 680 and 640, both on his native island of Paros and at Thasos, which was a colony of the former.

Plutarch places the **Pericles** and **Fabius Maximus** in the series of his biographies; they comprise the **tenth book** out of a sequence of 23. He lists three virtues shared by both men, **moderation**, **uprightness**, and the **ability to endure the follies of their peoples and their colleagues in office**. In fact, actual points of comparison between the two are rather slight. Quintus Fabius Maximus, surnamed *Cunctator* ('One who plays for time'), was five times consul and twice dictator during the Second Punic War, in the last part of the third century B.C. He resisted Hannibal's advances with a dogged, but rather unimaginative, persistence. He was also quite neurotic about being outshone by possible rivals.

Plutarch is rather hard-pressed to find parallels between him and Pericles. Fabius is described as 'magnanimous and leonine' (*Fabius* chap. 1). He is reminiscent of Pericles in possessing a 'spirit and dignity of character' that matched the needs of the time (*Fabius* chap. 3). On the other hand, although his speech was 'lofty' it was not naturally graceful or compelling. Both men were able to rein in a too-exuberant populace (*Comparison* 1), but they handled their political opponents in very different ways, as Plutarch admits (*Comparison* 3). There is a story of Hannibal's sparing Fabius' estates (*Fabius* chap. 7) that echoes—perhaps only fortuitously—an incident in Pericles' career (see chap. 33 below). The topic is taken up by P. Stadter, 'Plutarch's Comparison of Pericles and Fabius Maximus', *Greek, Roman and Byzantine Studies* 16 (1975) 77-85, esp. 79ff.

Chapter 3

For Pericles' family-tree, see Endnote F below. All Athenians were known by their name and the name of their deme (local district), and in fully formal circumstances by the name of their tribe as well.

The defeat of the Persian fleet off Mt. **Mycale**, on the Turkish coast across from Samos (479 B.C.), is described by Herodotus (9.96ff.), who mentions that the Athenian forces were commanded by Pericles' father, **Xanthippus**.

Herodotus is also the ultimate source for the information concerning Pericles' maternal great-uncle, **Cleisthenes**. In describing Cleisthenes' constitution as **admirably balanced**, Plutarch is using terms of analysis that came into favour with political theorists much later than Cleisthenes. Only with Aristotle and his followers did it become popular to analyze constitutions in terms of their blending or mixture of three main elements, monarchic, aristocratic and democratic.

By identifying **Agariste** as **the niece** of Cleisthenes the lawgiver, the translator is tacitly correcting a mistake by Plutarch, who makes her his granddaughter. The story of Agariste's dream before giving birth was well known (Herodotus 6.131). Aristophanes could not resist a farcical reference to it at *Knights* 1037: 'a lion . . . who will fight for the people with a multitude of mosquitoes'.

There are several Roman copies of Pericles' portrait-bust. According to G.M.A. Richter, these 'must all have been faithfully reproduced from the same Greek original', probably the statue set up on the Acropolis, which Pausanias mentions (1.25.1) and perhaps identical with a famous statue of Pericles by Cresilas (Pliny, *Natural Histories* 34.74; see Intro. above, sec. 3). (See Richter, *The Portraits of the Greeks* [London, 1965] I.104).

Plutarch accepts the common interpretation that Pericles was depicted with his helmet pushed back to hide **his head, which was rather long and out of proportion**. (Possibly, however, the pushed-back helmet was merely the sculptor's device to indicate that his subject was a general.) The *schinos* or *skilla* is the plant designated by botanists 'urginea maritima'; the term 'squill-headed' is applied to Pericles again in the citation from Cratinus in chap. 13 below.

The date of the *Cheirons*, or *Tutors*, is unknown. Its title derives from the chorus which was composed of multiple versions of Achilles' tutor, Cheiron. Its theme was the low level of morals and 'modern' music in contemporary Athens, not an unusual topic for the satirist in any age; in it Solon, recalled from the dead, complained that his laws were not being observed. In this citation (fragment 258 in Kassel and Austin, *Poetae Comici Graeci*) *Cronos* (or perhaps *Chronos*, 'Time', as in the manuscripts) and the abstraction *Stasis* (Faction, Party-strife) beget not Zeus but **the biggest tyrant**, who is, of course, Pericles, designated **Head-compeller** which in Greek by the change of just two letters parodies a standard Homeric epithet for Zeus, 'Cloud-gatherer'.

In *Nemesis* (frag. 118 Kassel-Austin), it is possible that the abstraction-goddess Nemesis represented Aspasia, seduced by Zeus (Pericles). Nemesis was thus a kind of double for Leda and some versions of the myth made Nemesis, not Leda, mother of Helen.

Zeus, the protector of foreigners and heads is a triple joke: pseudo-Homeric epithets are used to point up Pericles' tyrannical role, and perhaps also his patronage of foreign luminaries like Anaxagoras, while the Greek word *karanie* (*of heads*) is a pun on one of Zeus' traditional epithets, *keraunie* (of thunderbolts).

Telecleides, who is cited again in chap. 16 below, presented in a play whose title is not known a ludicrous travesty portraying Pericles, again in a Zeus-like posture, **sitting on the Acropolis** (which stands for Olympus); **the din of war** alludes probably to the stories, encountered elsewhere, that Pericles instigated the war against Sparta to cover up certain peccadilloes of himself or his associates. A room 'of so many couches' seems to have been a standard measurement of size; **big enough to hold eleven couches** is unusually large, since a nine- or ten-couch room is the biggest we hear of. Elsewhere Plutarch criticizes ostentatiously wealthy individuals for building rooms 'of thiry couches or more' (*Moralia* 679 B).

Eupolis was a strong rival to Aristophanes; with Cratinus, these

31

comprised the 'big three' of Old Comedy. *The Demes* was one of his most successful plays from which many citations survive. It was produced about 412 B.C., when the Athenian statesmen, including Pericles, who were summoned back from Hades to give advice on Athens' current problems, were long dead. (**The very head of those . . . below** seems to us a very bad pun.)

Chapter 4

Plutarch proceeds to a discussion of Pericles' 'teachers', a term used in a very loose sense, since these may have been only men with whom he was known to have associated. One of the preoccupations of later research was to establish who had influenced—put more formally, instructed—whom, and this chain of succession often included not only other philosophers but statesmen and politicians as well. It was also difficult for later scholars to accept that men of action had not had in their entourages professional advisors and 'resource persons' of various kinds, on the model of Alexander the Great. In Pericles' case it is unknown what (if any) evidence there was for the assertions made in this chapter and later in the *Life*.

The link with *Anaxagoras* and the latter's instruction in rigorous and abstract thinking is, as we have seen, as old as Plato. The author of the dialogue *Alcibiades I*, ascribed to Plato but probably not by him, adds the name of *Pythocleides* as one of Pericles' teachers (in ascribing this detail to *Aristotle* Plutarch either has misremembered, or he may be citing a now-lost work). Not much is known about Pythocleides of Ceos; one source calls him a 'Pythagorean' and says that he as a 'teacher of elevated music'. Interestingly Plato in *Protagoras* (316 D-E) lists him among Sophists who had to conceal their real talents, of which ordinary people were somewhat suspicious, behind 'screens' of other occupations. In Pythocleides' case it was presumably music, and Plato uses language similar to that applied to Damon here; one anonymous account even made Pythocleides the teacher of Damon.

There are several problems connected with **Damon**. First, it is not clear that this individual and the Damonides mentioned in chap. 9 below are two different people (see note there). Second, the date and real reason for his ostracism (if that actually happened and was not merely an invention of the comic stage) are problematic. It is clear from references in Plato and elsewhere that he was a respected, influential musician, and in the *Alcibiades I* (118c), whose dramatic date is 432 B.C., Pericles is said 'still' to be associating with him. He was held in high regard by Socrates, probably because of his theories concerning the influence of music on human behaviour. Plato in the *Republic* (424 C) quotes his dictum that 'the kinds of music cannot be changed without affecting the most important political *nomoi*', where there is a pun on *nomos*, 'tune' and 'law, custom'. Stories of his influence upon Pericles are as old as Isocrates who, in a speech written about 355 B.C., mentions him along with Anaxagoras and states that he was 'reputed to be the wisest of his day'. One *ostrakon* with the name Damon survives, and if the man actually was ostracized (he will have been one of the few non-politicians to be accorded this dubious distinction), it probably took place in the 440's, and perhaps as part of a campaign between by Pericles' supporters and his enemies, who included Thucydides son of Melesias, himself ostracized in 444/3 (mentioned in chaps. 6, 14 and 16 below). None of this can be considered certain, however, and some of it any rate may go back to the kind of comic situation to which Plutarch alludes in citing the line of Plato immediately below.

When Plutarch says that Pericles' teacher acted **as a masseur or trainer** to **an athlete**, he is using the kind of comparison of which he is extremely fond; throughout his works there is an abundance of metaphors from everyday life. (In the companion *Life*, Plutarch twice compares Fabius to a clever athlete and he once likens Fabius' opponent, Hannibal, to an athlete whose strength has been depleted —a point I owe to Prof. Sansone.)

The lines cited from **Plato, the comic dramatist** (often called 'Plato Comicus' to distinguish him from the philosopher) repeat the same joke as Cratinus had used in *Tutors* or *Cheirons*, referred to in the preceding chapter; Damon is the older, by implication somewhat disreputable, Svengali behind Pericles, like the centaur Cheiron to Achilles. Plato Comicus was a prolific and successful comic writer who worked in the last quarter of the fifth and early years of the fourth centuries; the passage here preserved may come from his play called *Sophists*.

Zeno the Eleatic is mentioned again in a biographical incident concerning Pericles at the end of chap. 5 below. He was a pupil of Parmenides of Elea, and was nicknamed 'the Eleatic Palamedes' (an inventive, even deceitful mythical figure) by Plato, who also reports the story that he charged the exorbitant sum of 100 minae to instruct Pericles. He is known for a series of ingenious paradoxes by which he attempted to show that space and time were infinitely divisible and that motion was illusory.

Timon of Phlius, a third-century Sceptic, besides associating with many important men of his day, such as Antigonus, Ptolemy Philadelphus and Aratus, was the author of tragedies, comedies and satyrdramas, as well as the *Silloi*, a satirical attack of philosophers in dactylic hexameters, from which these lines quoted by Plutarch derive.

Plutarch ends his chapter by returning to **Anaxagoras** and a brief account of some of his philosophical theories. He was called

Intelligence personified by **men of his time** because he made *Nous* (mind, intelligence) the dominating principle of the universe. A native of **Clazomenae** on the coast of Ionia, he owed his interest in natural phenomena and analysis of the basic physical constituents of matter to his forerunners in the Ionian school of philosophy. But he broke with them in positing a non-material substance as the basic explanation of the world. In his theory, Intelligence was the organizing principle that brought order out of primeval chaos and separated out the homogeneous parts, of which each thing contains a preponderance, along with other, heterogeneous parts. Plutarch refers to this as **the principle of law and order . . . which distinguishes . . . those substances which possess elements in common.**

In addition, Anaxagoras also interested himself in astronomy. He taught that the sun and celestial bodies were nothing but masses of molten metal ('incandescent stones'), a theory that got him into trouble with traditionalists and the superstitious, who believed that the heavenly bodies were divine; he was later prosecuted for impiety (see on chap. 32 below).

Chapter 5

The influence of Anaxagoras continues, even into Pericles' personal demeanour. Just as the pupil had **a composure of countenance that never dissolved into laughter** so Anaxagoras himself was alleged never to have laughed or even smiled. With his **serenity . . . which nothing could disturb while he was speaking**, compare the story told in chap. 8 below (and elsewhere) to illustrate that Pericles was extremely cautious in his use of words. These qualities impressed Demosthenes, we are told, who according to Plutarch 'sought to imitate the modulation of [Pericles'] speech and the dignity of his bearing' (*Life of Demosthenes* 9). Although Plutarch may overstate the theme of Pericles' 'Olympian' composure and self-possession, which in any case his enemies found nothing but offensive arrogance, there is something of this even in Thucydides' picture.

It is unknown from what source Plutarch got the story of Pericles' patiently allowing **himself to be abused and reviled for an entire day**; Themistocles was not so restrained (see his retort to the man from Seriphos, as told by Plutarch in his *Life of Themistocles*, chap. 18).

For further information about **Ion** of Chios see Intro. section 3. His praise of Cimon's **ease, good humour, and polished manner** (further praise at *Life of Cimon* chaps. 5, 9 and 16) probably comes from the *Sojourns*. He is cited for another detail critical of Pericles in chap. 28 below. For his work as a dramatist see note on the new **Omphale**, *chap. 24 below. For* **Zeno** see note on chap. 4 above.

Chapter 6

Plutarch continues the topic of Anaxagoras' influence. Besides his beneficial effects upon Pericles' powers of abstract thought and composed platform manner, he was widely believed to have communicated to him a practical scientific spirit that enabled him **to rise above . . . superstitious terror** (for an anecdote illustrating Pericles' freedom from superstition, see chap. 38 below). In the accounts of Cicero, Valerius Maximus and Quintilian, it is precisely Anaxagoras' astronomical teachings that enable Pericles to quell popular fears after a solar eclipse (see chap. 35 below, where Anaxagoras is not named).

The story about the **one-horned ram** does not occur elsewhere, and it is possible that it was invented not only to illustrate the difference between the scientific and the gullible attitudes to unusual natural occurrences, but also to heighten the sense of inevitability behind Pericles' rise to power. If so, **Lampon**, a well-known soothsayer and associate of Pericles, made an excellent representative of the superstitious side. 'He was the frequent butt of the contemporary comic poets for his hypocrisy, orthodoxy and greed' (Holden). Pericles named him one of the official founders of the colony to Thurii in 443 B.C. (see chap. 11 below), an act which is thought by many to have sealed the political downfall of **Thucydides** (hence the appropriateness of his being brought into the story here; more in chaps. 8, 11 and 14). Aristophanes could not resist a satirical shot at 'Thurii-priests' and other charlatans in *Clouds* (332), and Lampon was Cratinus' main target in *Runaway Women* (perhaps the colonists), of unknown date. Lampon's name was among the Athenian signatories of the armistice with Sparta in 421.

Plutarch begins and ends the chapter with a disquisition on superstition, a subject dear to his heart and to which he devoted a whole treatise (*Moralia* 164 E and following). His purpose is to counteract **ignorant wonder at the common phenomena of the heavens**, and he analyzes it in Aristotelian terms: superstition (literally, 'fear of demons') is the excess of which 'piety' is the mean and impiety or atheism the defect. Plutarch's argument presupposes the existence of God or Gods who sometimes at least show their benevolence to men through natural signs, or **divine portents**.

Chapter 7

This chapter is crucial in Plutarch's analysis of Pericles' rise to political power. Plutarch attempts to explain how it was that Pericles went against his own background (**rich . . . of a distinguished family**) and his own natural temperament (**thoroughly aristocratic**) to become an extremely successful popular leader. Plutarch's answer—and it seems to be very much of his own devising—was that Pericles saw a vacuum in the Athenian power-structure (**Aristeides was dead, Themistocles in exile**). One side of the dichotomy 'Aristocracy–Proletariat' was already filled (**Cimon . . . the idol of the aristocratic party**), so Pericles took the opposite tack and **decided to attach himself to the people's party . . . began to ingratiate himself with the people**.

This is an interesting construct (and Plutarch reiterates the point in chap. 9 below), but it will not stand up under closer inspection. For one thing, the polarization 'aristocrat' vs. 'populist', though it has behind it the authority of the *Constitution of Athens* ascribed to Aristotle, is largely an anachronism. Cimon, who expanded the Empire and beautified the city, was every bit as 'populist' as Pericles, and Pericles as much an aristocrat as Cimon (as Plutarch acknowledges). The cutting edge of the distinction came in foreign policy, and, as between Themistocles and Cimon, their attitudes to Sparta.

In addition, there is a hint of another explanation which is not easily harmonized with the one just considered, that Pericles made a conscious decision to carve for himself a piece of the political pie. According to this view, Pericles was secretly and at heart a demagogue all along, but did not dare show his true colours until late in his career because of **the fear of ostracism**. This seems to be a personal interpretation by Plutarch, and may be nothing more than speculation, as the related guess that Pericles was **afraid . . . of being suspected of aiming at a dictatorship** seems to be.

It is not clear what evidence, if any, Plutarch had for the allegation that Pericles **was considered to bear a distinct resemblance to the tyrant Pisistratus**. Possibly nothing more serious lies behind it than the barb aimed at Pericles and his friends by the comic poets that they acted like 'new Peisistratids' (see chap. 16). Who alive in (say) 465 B.C. would have been in a position to vouch for **the resemblance between the two** men? Even the tradition of Pisistratus' skill as an orator, which is encountered in certain late sources (see Cicero, *Brutus* 7.27 and 10.41) may be nothing more than a retrojection from Pericles' own position. Behind this lurks a vicious smear-campaign which can be seen in a fuller and uglier form in an anecdote told by Valerius Maximus (see Intro. sec. 3): an old man who as a youth had heard Pisistratus speak, when he heard the maiden speech in the Assembly by the young Pericles, cried out that the Athenians should beware because the manner of the two men's orations was so similar, and (Valerius or his source comments), he was right; 'for what difference was there between Pisistratus and Pericles except that the former wielded his tyranny with weapons and the latter without them?' (A more innocent version of this rhetorical commonplace is told by Plutarch elsewhere: an old man who, when young, had heard

Pericles speak encouraged Demosthenes, who had just suffered a reverse and was disheartened; he touched the young orator's hand and told him he resembled Pericles in natural ability [*Moralia* 795 C-D].) It also seems strange that Plutarch should attach to the topic of Pericles' **ingratiating himself with the people** his alleged aloofness. It is not immediately apparent that one who was letting the mask slip and revealing himself as a demagogue would **take care not to make himself too familiar**, except on the dubious principle that 'familiarity breeds contempt' (few modern politicians would take this as a practical technique of winning votes although exceptions, like de Gaulle, do come to mind). Plutarch repeats this account of a 'conversion' for political purposes in *Precepts of Statecraft*: 'he changed his physical comportment and his way of life, so that he walked more slowly, spoke in a moderate way, always showed a composed expression on his face, kept his hand inside his cloak and walked a single path—that leading to the speaker's platform and the council chamber' (*Moralia* 800C).

In the story of Pericles' early departure from the **wedding-feast** (Plutarch's source is unknown), the family connections plausibly suggested by J.K. Davies (*Athenian Properties Families* pp. 377-78) would make **Euryptolemus** Pericles' second cousin and a brother of Cimon's wife, Isodike (another arrangement would make Eurypto-lemus her son). In any case, the ruminations about **convivial occasions . . . breaking down the most majestic demeanour** are Plutarch's own, but something of a cliché ('in vino veritas').

The source of the quip about Pericles **reserving himself . . . for great occasions**, like the *Salamina*, is credited to **Critolaus**, a student and successor of Ariston of Ceos (whom Plutarch cites elsewhere) as head of the philosophical school founded by Aristotle. He made an impression as one of a delegation of Athenian intellectuals to Rome in 155 B.C., and wrote treatises on rhetoric, moral philosophy and history. Plutarch repeats the story at *Moralia* 811 C-D.

The *Salamina* was, along with Paralos (also the name of Pericles' son), one of Athens' two special despatch-boats, reserved for special and sometimes urgent missions; Thucydides tells how it had been sent to bring Alcibiades back from Sicily to stand trial in late 415 B.C. (A character in Aristophanes' *Birds* makes a similar joke when he asks the down-swooping and elaborately rigged Iris whether she is 'Paralos or Salamina'.)

That **Ephialtes** (mentioned also in chaps. 9, 10 and 16 below) was a mere front-man for Pericles was a story current as early as Aristotle's day. In *Politics* (1274a8) he says 'Ephialtes and Pericles docked the power of the Areopagus Council,' and a more full-bodied version of this relationship is given by Plutarch in his essay, *Precepts of Statecraft* (*Moralia* 812 C-D), where Ephialtes is listed, along with Lampon and two others, as members of the 'crew' of Pericles' Ship of

State (put differently, lackeys who were employed to do the necessary but often less pleasant tasks). It is equally possible that the removal of some of the judicial **power of the Council of the Areopagus** here referred to, which took place in 462/1 B.C., was the work solely or principally of Ephialtes (an otherwise unknown Archestratus is once mentioned as sharing in the legislation), and that Pericles' name became attached later by a biographical tradition that tried to turn him into a more rabid democrat than he in fact was. Somewhat less probably, Pericles might have been responsible for separate legislation, perhaps setting up a Board of '*Nomophylakes*', or Guardians of the Laws, who exercised a general supervision over the laws that had originally been exercised by the Areopagus. In any case, the exact nature of the powers stripped from the Areopagus on this occasion is unclear. The best, though somewhat brief, account is in the *Constitution of Athens*, where we read that Ephialtes 'took away all the additional privileges by virtue of which the Areopagus was the guardian of the state, and gave some to the (Boule of) 500, some to the popular assembly and some to the lawcourts' (25.2). What exactly these 'additional privileges' were cannot be determined; some have suggested that they included the screening of magistrates before they assumed office or an audit of their accounts afterwards, or the judicial procedure known as *eisangelia*.

The paraphrase from **Plato** at the end of the chapter, **poured out neat a full draught of freedom for the people and made them unmanageable** is from *Republic* (8.562 C-D); Plato uses the image of 'base wine-stewards in charge of the demos' and not of Ephialtes in particular.

The phrase **nibbled at Euboea and trampled on the islands** is cited from some unnamed comedy (Plutarch's text says as much: 'the comic writers say . . .', but this has unaccountably been omitted in the translation); the author may be the Telecleides cited in chaps. 3 and 16, although Eupolis applied the phrase 'obey the whip' to the subject city Chios in his play *Cities*. Aristophanes has a somewhat similar joke about Euboea, and also in connection with Pericles; two characters in *Clouds* are looking at a map of Greece and one says, 'Here's Euboea, look how flat and very long it stretches out,' and the other retorts, 'Of course, it was laid out flat by us and Pericles' (a reference to the suppression of the revolt there in 446 B.C.; see chaps 22 and 23 below).

Chapter 8

Plutarch is not yet through with the topic of Pericles' debt to **Anaxagoras**; the latter's lessons in **natural philosophy** gave **his (Pericles') oratory** a certain 'lift', and constituted 'an extra string to his bow' (Plutarch is fond of images from music; a study of his imagery lists 55 occurrences of such images and suggests that they are a legacy from the Pythagoreans and Plato). For Pericles' indebtedness to Anaxagoras Plutarch cites Plato (*Phaedrus* 270a) without, apparently, realizing that Plato is being more than a little satirical about Anaxagoras' 'elevation of reasoning,' for which Plato coins the term *meteōrologia*. Plutarch then returns to and expands the topic introduced in chap. 3, Pericles **the Olympian**, and speculates on the precise basis for the nickname. He concludes (quite sensibly) that it was probably **the combination of many qualities which earned him the name**. A character in Aristophanes' *Acharnians* (425 B.C.) says 'Olympian Pericles thundered and lightened and confounded Hellas' in anger at the Megarians for stealing some prostitutes from Aspasia's brothel (there is no evidence that the Megarians were ever involved in any such incident, or that Aspasia was a brothel-keeper (see Endnote D below).)

The phrase **wielding a terrible thunderbolt in his tongue** is generally taken as derived from an as yet unidentified comedy. Pericles' oratorical abilities get a left-handed compliment from Plato in the *Symposium* when Alcibiades says that when he 'heard Pericles and other good orators he recognized their qualities as speakers,' but that when he listened to Socrates he was moved to a bacchic frenzy and even to tears (*Symp.* 215e).

Plutarch will return to the topic of **Thucydides, the son of Melesias . . . a political opponent of Pericles for many years** in chaps. 11 and 14 below. There was a tradition that, when he was ostracised in 444/3 B.C., he went into exile in Sparta (although others said Thrace), and this anecdote may have this background as its (probably fictitious) setting, since **Archidamus II**, **king of Sparta** in the Eurypontid line, reigned from 469 to 427 B.C., and was known as a personal guest-friend of Pericles. He personally led the first two Peloponnesian invasions of Attica, in 431 and 430 B.C. (see chap. 33 below).

Thucydides' father **Melesias** was a celebrated and successful wrestling-coach who, as several references in Pindar's victory-odes show, had something of an international clientele. If the reference at Plato, *Meno* 94c, has a factual basis, the interest in wrestling continued in the family, for we are there told that Thucydides made his sons 'the best wrestlers in Athens'. It is possible that Plutarch or his source has given a garbled version of the story (also at *Moralia* 802 A), which probably referred to a metaphorical wrestling-match, not a real one. There is a similar joke in Aristophanes' *Knights* (571ff.) where the chorus of young aristocrats praise their fathers' indomitable bravery: 'If ever their shoulders touched the ground in any fight, they'd brush themselves off, deny they'd fallen, and join the wrestling again.'

The anecdote of Pericles' prayer that **no word might escape his lips . . . unsuited to the matter in hand** was a standard element in the tradition concerning Pericles' care (and pomposity) about his oratory; it is in Quintilian (see Intro. sec. 3), Plutarch tells it again in *Precepts of Statecraft* (*Moralia* 803 F), and it will recur in about 200 A.D. in Aelian's *Miscellaneous Stories* (where it has a more down-to-earth twist: '. . . no word that might irritate the people').

There was a debate among Roman writers on rhetoric whether or not Pericles had left any authentic speeches; Cicero says several times that he did, Quintilian is equally firm that the works passing under his name shortly before 100 A.D. were spurious, and this is Plutarch's view. Of **the decreees he proposed** (P.J. Rhodes believes that 'a collection of his decrees was made' [*A Commentary on the Aristotelian Athenaion Politeia*, p. 334]), traces can be found in chaps. 10, 17, 20, 25, 29, 30 and 34.

Aegina, 'that eyesore of the Peiraeus', was one of Pericles' most famous sayings, as is shown by Aristotle's citation in the *Rhetoric*, and Plutarch quotes it several times elsewhere; it refers to the fact that Aegina, though near enough to be seen from Peiraeus, had through her hostility caused Athens a good deal of trouble throughout her history.

Pericles' rather prudish rebuke to Sophocles, that a general **has to keep his eyes clean**, as well as his hands, is reported also by Cicero and Valerius Maximus. Since a story of similar purport is quoted elsewhere on the authority of Ion of Chios (see Intro. sec. 3), it is likely that his *Sojourns* was also Plutarch's source here. Pericles and Sophocles were colleagues in the Samian War, 441-440 B.C. The citation preserved by **Stesimbrotus** (107 F 9 Jacoby) from Pericles' **funeral oration for those who had fallen in the war against Samos** (which is mentioned again in chap. 28 below) is the longest specimen of Pericles' oratory, if we exclude the speeches attributed to him by Thucydides, which many scholars believe are compilations of arguments used by Pericles on more than one occasion, and have in any case been reworked to fit the historian's own style.

Chapter 9

Plutarch opens the chapter with Thucydides' famous characterization of **Pericles' administration . . . 'democracy in name, but in practice government by the first citizen'** (2.65.9). He immediately counters with the charges levelled against his democratic measures by such critics as Plato and probably also Theopompus, who complained that because of payments for public service allegedly instituted by Pericles the ordinary citizens of Athens **fell into bad habits and became extravagant and undisciplined instead of frugal and self-sufficient**. This is, of course, the usual conservative complaint against any measure of state aid or 'social security', that the ordinary man thereby 'loses initiative' and would be better off 'doing it for himself'.

Thus Plato: '. . . Pericles made the Athenians lazy, cowards, blabber-mouths and money-grubbers, by first establishing pay for public service' (*Gorgias* 515e).

Of the specific measures mentioned here and later in the chapter, only **allotment of lands belonging to subject peoples** (the so-called 'cleruchies', to which Plutarch returns in chap. 11 below) and payment of two obols per day for jury-duty are demonstrably attributable to Pericles, the latter having been instituted around 460 B.C. It is possible but unproven that he was also responsible, later in his career, for introducing payment of three obols per day to soldiers and sailors on active duty, and a drachma per day to Councillors. Payment to attend the Assembly and **allowances for the public festivals** were not instituted until after 400. Of course it could be argued that since he had set the process in motion he was morally responsible for the last developments as well. Plutarch alludes to Pericles' policy of providing public festivals and entertainments also at Moralia 818 D. (See further Endnote B, below.)

Plutarch now re-opens the question of Pericles' motive, which he touched on in chap. 7. These demagogic measures are explained as introduced to counteract **Cimon's reputation** for largesse, a means by which Pericles himself might **win the favour of the people**. The public benefactions of Cimon mentioned here and in the *Life of Cimon* chap. 10 (as well as by Nepos, *Cimon* 4) derive, along with others in a similar vein, directly from Theopompus, who maintained that Cimon was in turn trying to match the reputation of Peisistratus. They read like gross exaggeration and in at least one particular did not go unchallenged in fourth-century historical research: in the *Constitution of Athens* and again by Aristotle's colleague and successor Theophrastus, the detail regarding free fruit-picking on Cimon's estates was corrected to read 'Cimon's fellow-demesmen, the Lakiadai', not **any Athenian who needed it** or **anyone who wished** ('even strangers' according to the *Life of Cimon* chap. 10).

According to the *Constitution of Athens* (27.4) Pericles was merely acting on the advice of **Damonides of the deme of Oa**, who may be the same man as the Damon mentioned in chap. 4 above (or possibly the text here should be altered to 'Damon son of Damonides'), to 'give the masses their own'. It is not known whether Plutarch is still drawing on his anti-Periclean source or whether he has made the connection himself between these popular measures and the **attack on the Council of the Areopagus**, to which he had already alluded in chap. 7.

Plutarch attributes to Pericles a further, personal, motive: **since he had never been appointed by lot** to the archonship and **because he had been excluded** (it is misleading to say, as Plutarch does later, that the archonships **had traditionally been filled by lot**; this change had only been introduced in 487 B.C.). Plutarch is quite correct, however, in his explanation that **membership of the Areopagus** was only open to **men who had acquitted themselves well** in the archonship, that is, who had passed the official scrutiny upon ending their year in office.

Plutarch closes the chapter with a rumination on the fickleness of the Athenian electorate (which is to say that the Athenians were no different from voters the world over, and in any period of history). In spite of Cimon's high breeding (**second to none . . . in birth**) and the largesses already alluded to; in spite of **brilliant victories over the Persians**, especially that at the Eurymedon river in about 468 B.C. (see *Life of Cimon* chaps. 12-13, derived from Thucydides 1.100.1, with embellishments by Aristotle's nephew, Callisthenes); in spite of his beautification of the city (at the end of chap. 13 of *Cimon* Plutarch lists the south retaining wall of the Acropolis, the foundations of the Long Walls to Peiraeus, plane trees in the Agora and improvements to the Academy), his political enemies secured his ostracism on grounds that he was **a friend of Sparta**, a fact which Cimon took no trouble to hide; he had called on the Athenians to render assistance to their 'yoke-mate', as he incautiously called Sparta, at the time of the Helot revolt (about 464 B.C.; Thucydides 1.101, 103), having previously revealed his personal preferences by naming one of his sons 'Lakedaimonios'. When the Spartans humiliatingly turned away the Athenian contingent, probably out of fear that their own troops would become 'contaminated' by the Athenians' revolutionary ideas, Cimon's enemies struck and he was ostracized. Who precisely these 'enemies' were Plutarch does not specify here, although he implies that part of the explanation lay in **the strength of Pericles' hold over the people**; in the *Comparison* of Pericles and Fabius Maximus 30 (3) he explicitly attributes responsibility to Pericles.

Chapter 10

That Cimon was recalled after only five years of the ten-year period of ostracism had elapsed was the view of Theopompus (Jacoby 115 F 88), and some modern scholars accept this, in spite of the silence of Thucydides and the implication of a remark by Plato (*Gorgias* 516d6) that Cimon remained away the full ten years. Even if this were so, Plutarch's highly coloured account of Cimon's presence at, but non-participation in the battle against the Spartans and their allies at *Tanagra* in Boeotia in midsummer 457 B.C. is suspect. Both Cimon and Pericles play stock roles (similar, in fact, to the antagonists of an earlier generation, Aristeides and Themistoeles): the ultra-patriot rebuffed by the selfish and partisan politician, who, when he sees that he has thus alienated the people's sympathies, does a volte-face and proposes **the decree to recall his opponent** (Plutarch is our only source for this detail).

The additional, even more romanticizing story that Pericles proposed the decree for Cimon's recall only after **a secret agreement had been reached . . . with the help of Elpinice, Cimon's sister**, probably derives from Stesimbrotus, who is named in the *Life of Cimon* for the account which Plutarch repeats there (chap. 14) of Elpinice's intervention with Pericles, who was prosecutor when **Cimon was being tried for his life on a charge of treason** after the Thasos campaign in 463 B.C. Pericles' role as prosecutor is also mentioned in the *Const. of Athens* ascribed to Aristotle (27.1). (In *The Life of Cimon*, Plutarch specifies the charge: it was alleged that Cimon had accepted a bribe from the King of Macedon not to follow up his success with an invasion of Macedonia.) It seems even less credible that Pericles should have allowed Cimon's sister to dictate the conditions of recall as well, that **Cimon should sail with an expedition** against Persia **and should take command abroad, while Pericles should have supreme authority at home**. This sounds more like a misunderstanding of some comic writer's absurd fantasy than sober history. In any case, even if there was something to the story of a deal between Pericles and Cimon, whereby the latter should take command abroad, while Pericles should have supreme authority at home, this is wrongly placed on Plutarch's chronology, for no such division of labour becomes evident until about 450 B.C. when Cimon did in fact, as Thucydides confirms (1.112.2), sail with an expedition of 200 ships to attempt to reduce the territory of the king of Persia. And this, of course, could just as easily have been after Cimon's return from a normal, ten-year period of ostracism. The story of an agreement between the two men to share responsibility occurs also at *Moralia* 812 F.

On the other hand, there is no reason to doubt that **Pericles had been chosen as one of the ten public prosecutors** at Cimon's trial in 463 B.C. and that, for whatever reason, Pericles went easy on Cimon, who was acquitted. Plutarch adequately refutes the charge, reported by Idomeneus (Jacoby 338 F 8) that **Pericles arranged the assassination of . . . Ephialtes** (for whom see chaps. 7 and 9 above). The *Constitution of the Athenians* (25.4) records the name of Ephialtes' alleged assassin, **Aristodicus of Tanagra**, but without mentioning Pericles.

Cimon's death . . . during his campaign in Cyprus occurred, on the chronology derived from Thucydides' account (1.112.4), in 450-449 B.C.

Chapter 11

Plutarch uses misleading terms to describe the political battle between **Thucydides**, son of Melesias, as leader of the **aristocratic**

party, (the **party of the few** later in the chapter) and Pericles, the arch-democrat. Although there may have been differences of political outlook, there is no evidence for hard-and-fast political parties, consistently committed to a political program or 'platform'.

For Thucydides, see above chaps. 6 and 8, and 14 and 16 below. In describing him as a **relative of Cimon** Plutarch follows *Ath. Pol.* 28.2, using a word that generally denotes a marriage-connection; according to J.K. Davies, 'no decision on the exact form of the family relationship is possible on the present evidence' (*Athenian Properties Families* p. 232). Plutarch may base his description **less of a soldier . . . but better versed in forensic business** on nothing more than that the sources did not record any particularly memorable military exploits of his, but rather emphasized his opposition to Pericles in the Assembly. It is difficult to know what evidence (if any) there was for Thucydides' **separating and grouping** (the aristocrats) **in a single body**.

The scheme which Plutarch takes over (or perhaps has himself devised) has Pericles consciously employing 'demagogic' means to counter Thucydides' influence. This fits well with the picture of him as a latter-day and unofficial 'monarch' or 'tyrant', for this is what was generally believed about why historical tyrants like Periander and Pisistratus undertook elaborate building and public-works projects (so, too, in chap. 12: 'should not be paid for sitting about and doing nothing'). Some scholars believe that this basically negative picture of Pericles' motives goes back to Theopompus (on whom see Intro. sec. 3.), who, however, is not named in the *Life of Pericles*. The phrase **entertaining the people like children with elegant pleasures** appears to come from some lost comedy ('Porson's law is violated', as Prof. Sansone remarks).

That Pericles was responsible for sending out **sixty triremes . . . every year . . . for eight months** has been doubted, on grounds that the costs involved would have been prohibitively expensive, even for a city with Athens' large imperial revenues. The information about Pericles' settlements abroad, on the other hand, seems to derive from a trustworthy source (although the settlement on **Naxos** has also been credited to Tolmides, who is mentioned in chap. 16 below). The dates of these ventures are not quite certain. **Thurii** can be dated c. 443. Scholars assign the others to the period between 453 and 447 B.C. Plutarch returns to the settlement at the Chersonese in chap. 19 below. Thurii, sent out with great fanfare and apparently as a panhellenic venture, although under Athens' sponsorship, features an all-star cast of settlers: the soothsayer Lampon (mentioned in chap. 6 above and by other ancient authorities), Herodotus the historian, Protagoras the philosopher, who was said to have made laws for the new colony, and a young Syracusan émigré who later returned to Athens and earned a reputation as a speech-writer, Lysias.

Plutarch ends the chapter by assigning motives: **relieved the city of . . . idlers and agitators** once more shows Pericles imitating the tyrants of old and is perhaps only conjectural. The two principal benefits, a rise in **the standards of the poorest classes** and **garrisons among the allies**, were no doubt Pericles' main reasons for these undertakings.

Chapter 12

For Plutarch, the focus of opposition to Pericles at this period, just after 450 B.C., was his elaborate scheme for the **construction of temples and public buildings**, and this is no doubt correct. Although Thucydides son of Melesias is not named again in this chapter, he (or someone very like him) must be the opponent whose charges against Pericles are reported here. It is interesting that Plutarch begins his discussion with what may be a conscious echo of Thucydides' comment (1.10) that appearances in this respect may deceive: Sparta's real power would be underestimated on the basis of what would in after ages be visible of her buildings and Athens' strength would be conjectured to be twice as great as it really was.

The act of **transferring from Delos** the imperial treasury is generally dated by historians c. 454 B.C., just before the start of the recorded transfers of one sixtieth of the allies' **contributions** each year from the League treasury to the Treasury of Athena in the Parthenon. When Pericles' critic refers to these contributions as **extorted from them by force for the war against the Persians**, he is taking the same line as Thucydides and some other ancient writers who saw these payments as the main irritant in Athens' relations with her allies, and the reason for the defection of many members of the Alliance. It is not clear whether the vivid picture of Athens' using these monies to tart herself up like **some vain woman decking herself out** is Plutarch's own invention. (Plutarch alludes to Pericles' use of the tribute monies to adorn Athens also at *Moralia* 343 D, and again, more briefly, at 348 C–D.)

Pericles' answer is couched in harder and more callous tones, but it is exactly the same justification as Thucydides provided in the 'Funeral Speech': 'In [Athens'] case alone, no invading enemy is ashamed at being defeated, and no subject can complain of being governed by people unfit for their responsibilities. Mighty indeed are the marks and monuments of our empire which we have left. Future ages will wonder at us, as the present age wonders at us now' (2.41, trans. by Rex Warner). It should be noted that if this speech of Pericles which Plutarch reports here really was delivered, and if he gave as a justification of continuing the allies' tribute-payments that the Athenians **kept the Persians away**, this would refute once and for all the theory that a peace treaty had been signed with Persia c. 449 B.C., the so-called 'Peace of Callias' (see Endnote C, 'Some Disputed Documents'). For Pericles' claim that his building program **transform[ed] the whole people into wage-earners** and for the actual **immense public works and plans for buildings**, see below, Endnote B. There is no reason to doubt that one of Pericles' main objectives was that **those who stayed at home . . . should be enabled to enjoy a share of the national wealth.**

The chapter closes with a splendid catalogue of the various materials and crafts employed, and with a series of graphic metaphors that are probably Plutarch's own (**like a general with an army . . . as an instrument obeys the hand, or the body the soul**).

Chapter 13

After reporting the anecdote involving the two noted fifth-century painters **Zeuxis** and **Agatharchus** (also at Moralia 94 E- F; Valerius Maximus 3.7 ext. 1 tells a similar story of Euripides), Plutarch launches into a rhapsodic appreciation of Athens' imperial buildings. Although it may be an exaggeration to say that **they were created in so short a span** (the Parthenon was begun in 447 and not finally completed until 433, and some projects like the Athena Nike temple were unfinished at Pericles' death), it is hard to imagine a more glowing eulogy than **a beauty which seemed venerable the moment it was born . . . a youthful vigour which makes them appear to this day as if they were newly built.**

From affectionate admiration for the Periclean achievement, Plutarch settles into some specifics about the designers. We must accept his identification of **Pheidias** as **supervisor of the whole enterprise** (Plutarch uses the term *episkopos* which may, but need not, denote an official post); there is more gossip about his relations with Pericles in chap. 31 below. Of the other artists, **Callicrates** and **Ictinus** worked together, or perhaps in succession, on the Parthenon, and the fact that only Ictinus' name is found in some ancient accounts may show that he had the lion's share. Although antiquity remembered him mainly as architect of the superb temple of Apollo at Bassae in the Peloponnese, his name is also mentioned in connection with **the temple of initiation at Eleusis**, about whose design Plutarch is remarkably well informed (**architrave** denotes the series of blocks immediately above the columns, **frieze** the sculptured band directly above that). Athens had long had a vested interest in Eleusis, about 12 miles to the north and west of the city. The local priesthoods and the cults of the vegetation goddess Demeter and her daughter Persephone were incorporated into the civic and religious life of Athens probably not long before 700 B.C., and there is evidence of structural building there of a shrine or viewing-place for those who were to be initiated, or received into, the 'mysteries' from the mid-sixth century. By far the most elaborate structure is that described here, for which, along with the Parthenon, Pericles acted as 'super-intendent', according to Strabo (9.1.12; C395). Its main viewing-space, designed with rows of seats on all four sides, measured approximately 175 feet square. Virtually nothing is known of the architects **Coroebus**, **Metagenes** and **Xenocles** beyond the information given here. See, in general, G.E. Mylonas **Eleusis and the Eleusinian Mysteries** (Princeton University Press, 1961) pp. 113ff., with illustrations. (Prof. A.L. Robkin has convinced me that the phrase translated here **crowned it with the lantern over the shrine** really means 'placed a viewing-window on top of the shrine'.)

There are problems in respect of Plutarch's report of the **third Long Wall,** Socrates' alleged attendance when **Pericles propose[d] the decree,** and **Cratinus'** apparently satirical reference. Not all of them have been satisfactorily solved. Plutarch alludes to the remark made by Socrates in Plato's *Gorgias* (455e), that he 'heard Pericles making a proposal about the "Middle" Wall'. According to Thucydides (1.107.1, 108.3), the building of the Long Walls which joined Peiraeus to the upper city, and hence made the two into a single unit, took place between 459 and 457 , when Socrates was not yet into his teens. On the other hand Gomme (*Comm. on Thuc.* vol. I, p. 312 n.3) cites an inscription of 443-2 referring to 'wall-builders' in connection with the Parthenon accounts, and this would be a suitable time for Callicrates to be involved in both projects (note that Plutarch says simply 'Long Wall', 'third' being an addition of the translator); in any case this is the earliest for Socrates, who was born in 469 B.C., to have been able to hear Pericles speaking on the subject. Nor is it clear exactly what Cratinus is making fun of (Plutarch quotes the passage, frag. 326 Kassell-Austin, again at *Moralia* 351 A). Possibly by 443, when the Athenians thought they had done with wall-building, Pericles came up with his proposal for an additional—perhaps more easily defensible—wall between the other two, and Cratinus for his own comic purposes satirized this as a mere ·ontinuation of the earlier scheme.

It is possibly significant that Vitruvius (*On Architecture* 5.9) ascribes the building of the **Odeon** to Themistocles, who is there said to have used 'ships' masts and yard-arms from the Persian spoils'. Since in many respects Pericles continued and brought to fruition his predecessor's policies, it is possible that the project had been drafted or was even begun by Themistocles. Very little remains of the actual building, which became famous for the numerous internal columns in the design. It stood to the southeast of the theatre of Dionysus, and was used for musical recitals and for some of the preliminaries of the dramatic competitions. [See J.G. Frazer, *Pausanias' Description of*

Greece (London 1913, repr. 1965) v. II, pp. 219-21; J. Travlos, *Pictorial Dictionary of Ancient Athens* (N.Y. 1971) 387-391; J.A. Davison, *From Archilochus to Pindar* (London 1968) 48-54.]

Cratinus' comedy, *The Thracian Women*, whose Chorus was composed of women celebrating the outlandish rites of the Thracian goddess Bendis, has been plausibly dated between 435 and 430 B.C. In the lines from it that Plutarch quotes Pericles' elongated head is referred to, the joke being emphasized by the reference to him—obscured by the translation—as 'wearing the Odeon on his head, now that the "clay tile" has passed by'. The term 'tile' is ambiguous, for it can mean either a roof-tile (fallen from the Odeon) or the pot fragments used in voting for ostracisms. Scholars have generally seen a reference to the removal of Pericles' opponent, Thucydides son of Melesias, in 444/3 B.C., mentioned at the end of chap. 14 below.

The **Panathenaic Festival** was celebrated in honour of the city's patron goddess, Athena, each year in mid-summer. Every fourth year an especially magnificent celebration was held, the 'Great' Panathenaea. Torch races, a regatta, athletic contests and various other competitions were held. It was to the four-yearly festival that Athens' allies and colonies were expected to send offerings to be carried in the solemn procession that wound through the city; these items, including a robe specially woven for the occasion, were presented to the image of the goddess in her ancient temple on the Acropolis. (All this is depicted on the frieze, or continuous band of sculpture, from the Parthenon, now in the British Museum.)

Plutarch is in error in stating that a **musical contest** was made **part of the Panathenaic Festival** only under Pericles, for such contests go back at least to the sixth century. Plutarch's source possibly drew a wrong inference from the decree naming Pericles as **one of the stewards** who made arrangements for the festival (in the fourth century these were a panel of ten and were allotted), which may have been held in a specially magnificent way to inaugurate the Odeon. Alternatively, there was a break in these competitions earlier in the fifth century, and they were restored by Pericles who in either case is signalling his patronage of the arts in the grand manner, like the family of the tyrant Pisistratus.

The **Propylaea**, or huge temple-like entranceway to the Acropolis, under construction from 437 to 433 B.C. and left unfinished, must have amazed and delighted its original visitors as it does modern-day tourists to Athens. Pericles was criticized by the fourth century politician Demetrius of Phaleron (see Intro., sec. 3) for the vast sums expended on a 'mere' gateway (details in Endnote B below). There were other versions of this story of Pericles' cure of the injured workman (see Intro., sec. 3.), but they are all intended to point the same moral: the gods smiled on and took special measures to protect Pericles' building program and all connected with it. The base of **the**

bronze statue of Athena the Healer was found during excavations of the Propylaea; it records the sculptor's name, Pyrros, and the fact that it was an official dedication by 'the Athenians'. The temple's crowning glory, **the great golden statue of Athena**, was completed and dedicated in 438/7; for details of its construction, see n. on chap. 31 below. Plutarch then returns to the topic of Pheidias' general supervision of the whole Acropolis building project. His account trails off in a series of scandalous but amusing tales, which read more like satire than sober history, and probably have no more to back them up than the fevered imaginings of the **comic poets**, to whom Plutarch here refers. The 'charge' is similar to that brought against Aspasia (ch. 32 beginning; also, as it happens, by a comic poet). Plutarch cannot resist recounting these spicy tit-bits, even if he only half-believes them, as is indicated by his rather pious disclaimer (**foul slanders against their betters**). **Menippus** is named elsewhere (*Moralia* 812 D) in a list of those used by Pericles as agents or 'front men' for his various activities, in Menippus' case, military ventures. **Pyrilampes** (the translation is to be corrected) was the second husband of Plato's mother; he was wounded and taken prisoner at the battle of Delium in 424 B.C. and several contemporary authorities mention his son Demos, who was famed for his good looks and his peacocks (his father probably introduced them to Athens after an embassy to Persia referred to by Plato at *Charmides* 158a; see in general D.M. MacDowell's n. on Aristoph. *Wasps* 98). A late source says that Pyrilampes was prosecuted for murder by Pericles at a trial before the Areopagus, with a Thucydides—probably the son of Melesias—speaking for the defense. The result was an acquittal. (The whole story sounds unhistorical.)

The **charge that Pericles seduced his son's wife**, made by **Stesimbrotus** (*FGrHist* 107 F 10b; see Intro., sec. 3.), is rejected here with a certain amount of feigned shock; it recurs again in chap. 36 below. The chapter closes with some sensible remarks about the difficulties of arriving at historical truth, even by contemporaries, whose view may be distorted by **envy or private hatred** or (worse) **the desire to flatter**.

Chapter 14

Pericles' **gesture in the grand manner** might be dismissed either as empty boasting or (more probably) a biographical fiction, were it not for the survival of a fragmentary inscription, the so-called 'Spring-house Decree', making arrangements for the upkeep of the city's public fountains (improvements in the public water-supply had also been the concern of the Pisistratid family). Towards the end of what survives on the stone [Fornara 117] there is a motion to thank Pericles and his sons Paralos and Xanthippus, but to pay for the waterworks from the city's tribute. The implication is that Pericles offered to finance the project himself, perhaps to get work started or to cow opposition of the sort referred to by Plutarch in these chapters.

The **ostracism** of Pericles' **rival**, Thucydides son of Melesias, is to be dated 444/3 B.C. In the 'Comparison of Pericles and Fabius', printed as a continuation of the *Life of Fabius*, Plutarch returns to the partisan spirit with which Pericles engineered the removal of his opponents, the 'noble and aristocratic' Cimon and Thucydides (*Fabius 30 = Comparison 3*).

Chapter 15

Except for brief references to two of his favourite sources, Plato and Thucydides, the bulk of this chapter seems to be Plutarch's own analysis. His main point, which he makes with a profusion of metaphors almost certainly of his own devising, is that, with all opposition effectively removed, Pericles could now lay aside his 'demagogic' mask (**ready to give way to** [the people's] **caprices; somewhat . . . indulgent leadership**) and become fully and firmly what he wanted to be all along, a true statesman. The totality of the control exercised by Pericles is emphasized by the catalogue of powers he **now proceeded to bring under his own control**, almost a prose rendering of the passage from Telecleides cited in the next chapter, and by the revealing description of Pericles' statesmanship as **aristocratic, even regal** (cf., later in the chapter, **more power . . . than many a king and tyrant**). Of course, this power was not entrusted to Pericles in any absolute or unconditional way; each campaign, each colony, each building project had to be sold to the popular assembly (and defended or justified, if it proved less than completely successful) in open and continuous debate, **by rational argument and persuasion**.

Plutarch alludes to the discussion of the power of **rhetoric** and its definition as **the art of working upon the souls of men** (*psychagōgia*) **by means of words**, as formulated by **Plato** in the dialogue *Phaedrus* (261a, cf. 271c-d; the dangers of unscrupulous use of this power are discussed in *Gorgias*). What saved Pericles from being a mere manipulator of mob emotions was **the confidence he enjoyed** because of his **whole course of life**, but particularly as one **completely indifferent to bribes**. This point (which Thucydides has Pericles himself include in his definition of a statesman [2.60.5-6]) and Pericles' skill at alternately **curbing** the people or **raising their hopes**, Plutarch has taken directly from **Thucydides** (2.65), with an acknowledgement.

Plutarch employs a variety of metaphors in this spirited chapter:

music, medicine, horsemanship, the sea. There may be an unconscious reminiscence of Plato's analogous use of imagery or parable to illustrate abstract points, e.g. the Ship-of-State metaphor in the **Republic** (488a-e), where the foolish sailors, unlike the True Pilot, insist that the rudder be turned over to them, in spite of their ignorance of the art of steering! Plutarch compares Pericles to a helmsman of a ship also in chap. 33 below.

Pericles, unlike other Athenian politicians who allegedly enriched themselves by holding public office, was reputed actually to have left to his children an estate smaller than that which he inherited from his father (so Isocrates *Orat.* 8.126). Contrast Pericles' own comment in the 'Funeral Oration': 'to the inheritance [that our fathers] had received they added all the empire we have now' (Thucydides 2.36.2). Plutarch returns to the point about Pericles' imperviousness to bribes in the *Comparison*; he 'never took anything from those who offered' (*Fabius* 30 [3]).

Chapter 16

It is not known which of the *comic poets*, or in what context, nicknamed Pericles' circle '**the new Pisistratids**'. The joke is of a piece with the absurd claim, reported in chap. 7 above, that Pericles bore a distinct resemblance to the tyrant Pisistratus. The whole motif sounds like a fantastic fiction based on Thucydides' observation that, because of Pericles' prestige and virtually unchallengeable position, 'power was really in the hands of the first citizen' (2.65.9, trans. R. Warner).

The citation from an unnamed play of **Telecleides** (see chap. 3 above) is very valuable, for it comically applied to Pericles terms for total and absolute power generally reserved for the gods. '**Cities' walls to build or to pull down**' may refer specifically to the punishment meted out to Samos in 439 B.C. after her unsuccessful rebellion (Thucydides 1.117.3), or more generally to Athens' treatment of her recalcitrant allies.

It is not clear what basis there was for the statement that for **forty years Pericles held the first place among men**; (forty was a conventional figure; cf. Cicero *On the Orator* 3.138). His first dated public appearance was sponsorship of Aeschylus' play, *The Persians*, in 472 B.C., but he is not mentioned as involved in politics until the late 460's. His **fifteen year continuous . . . tenure** of the generalship is probably to be dated 443/2 to 429/8 (though removed from office and fined in the latter year, he was very soon restored to power; see end of chap. 35 below and Thucydides 2.65.3-4).

In the list of other prominent men in whose company Pericles **held the first place** the name of Leocrates has been unaccountably omitted by the translator; he is mentioned by Thucydides (1.105.2) as general in the naval campaign against Aegina in 458 and Plutarch refers again to his success as a general in *Comparison* 1 (Myronides and Leocrates are named as colleagues of Aristeides at *Aristeides* 20). **Myronides** was active in the events of the so-called 'First Peloponnesian War', winning victories against the Corinthians in the Megarid and against the Boeotians at Oinophyta in 457 (Thucydides 1.105 and 108). Two military undertakings of **Tolmides**, one a success, the other a total failure, are noted in chaps. 18 and 19 below.

Plutarch next digresses to illustrate Pericles' close-fistedness (the story may come from Stesimbrotus, who is cited for the more scurrilous gossip connecting Pericles and his son Xanthippus' wife in chaps. 13 and 36). By selling off **each year's produce in a single sale** and using his agent **Evangelus**—not mentioned elsewhere—to buy supplies as needed, he was able to keep close track of his expenses, and his in-laws thus had no opportunity to 'pad the accounts'.

Anaxagoras, who has not been heard from since chap. 8, returns as the type of the 'unwordly' abstract thinker, and serves as a counter-example to Pericles' meticulous bookkeeping. The story that he **let his land . . . be grazed by sheep** is repeated at *Mor.* 831 F. The earliest surviving report that he neglected his property appears to be Plato, *Hippias maior* 283a; he was also reported as providing an example of magnanimity by turning over family property to his relatives, because he couldn't be bothered to look after it (Diogenes Laertius 2.3.6-7).

The report that Pericles used his wealth to give **help to many of the poorer citizens** may be sheer conjecture. In any case it sits uneasily with the version in chap. 9 above, where we saw Pericles having to use disbursements of public monies to counteract Cimon's bountiful expenditures from his private fortune. The anecdote with which the chapter ends, Pericles visiting the self-neglecting Anaxagoras on his death-bed, also seems inconsistent with the account in chap. 32 below of how Pericles 'smuggled him out of the city' rather than have him stand trial. Anaxagoras has the last word, and Pericles is cast as the typical wealthy patron oblivious of his obligations to an impoverished protégé.

Chapter 17

In recording the terms of the decree Plutarch uses technical language, which has suggested to some scholars that he had a documentary source, perhaps the collection of 'Periclean Decrees' mentioned by him in chap.8 (see note there). This does not in itself guarantee the Decree's authenticity, and I personally find the clauses suspiciously detailed and precise-sounding—like good historical fiction. What makes the case particularly hard to evaluate is that the proposed

Panhellenic Congress never took place; it was a non-event. Pericles must in any case have known (or suspected) that the Spartans would not agree to attend a gathering which by its nature bore witness to Athenian initiative. Or perhaps he was just looking for an opportunity to show up Sparta as inward-looking and unco-operative?

For the vexing problems connected with this proposal to summon a Panhellenic **congress at Athens**, see Endnote C, 'Some Disputed Documents'.

Chapter 18

Pericles is cast as the supercautious military commander, and in this role **Tolmides'** disastrous invasion of Boeotia in 447 B.C., ending with his death **near Coronea** (an engagement in which Alcibiades' father Cleinias also fell), makes a useful contrast. (Prof. Sansone points out to me that Plutarch similarly emphasizes the contrast between Fabius 'the Delayer' and his impetuous lieutenant M. Minucius, [see *Fabius* chaps. 5, 8, 12] and that this latter opposition may be influencing Plutarch's account here. Plutarch may have been further induced to exaggerate the differences between the two men by the meaning of Tolmides' name, 'He who dares'.) Plutarch adds nothing to Thucydides' account of the disaster (1.113, where the size of the force is also given as 1,000), except the report that Pericles tried to **restrain Tolmides and dissuade him from going**. In the *Comparison* 3 (= *Fabius* 30) Tolmides is given as an example of one who suffered for 'breaking away from Pericles' guidance', by an almost divine retribution. Gomme in his discussion of this campaign notes that since Pausanias (1.27.5) reports that a commemorative statue of Tolmides and his seer Theainetos was set up on the Acropolis, 'he was not repudiated for his failure' (*Commentary on Thucydides* vol. I, p. 339). Pericles' saying regarding **Time, the most experienced counsellor of all** (others such in chap. 8 above) is not reported elsewhere.

Chapter 19

In the next chapter-and-a-half Plutarch narrates, at some length but not (apparently) sequentially, Pericles' three most renowned overseas ventures, his leading of settlers to the Chersonese, the expedition to the Corinthian Gulf and Acarnania, and his peacekeeping mission to the Black Sea. Only one of these, the voyage along the shore of the Corinthian Gulf, is mentioned by Thucydides, which is perhaps why only this can be given a secure date.

Athens had been interested in the Chersonese since at least the mid sixth century, when the elder Miltiades led settlers there and set up a kind of private fiefdom. At some time in the 460's Cimon had to pacify the area once again and make it safe for Athenian habitation (Plutarch, *Cimon* 14). Now Pericles goes a step further, apparently in person leading 1,000 settlers (also mentioned in chap. 11 above), and building a fortification across **the neck of the isthmus . . . from sea to sea** (similar fortifying activity is ascribed also to the elder Miltiades and to the Spartan Dercyllidas in the early fourth century, so Pericles' solution was not a definitive one). Scholars generally place the settlement in the early 440's.

Tolmides' expedition to the Corinthian Gulf, which Pericles appears to be trying to emulate, took place in 456/5 and was genuinely a circumnavigation; Thucydides (1.108.5) reports it as a striking success, which involved, among other achievements, setting fire to the Spartan dockyards at Gytheum. It is not quite correct to refer to Pericles' venture, which is to be dated c. 453 B.C., as a **voyage round the Peloponnese**, since Plutarch himself, following Thucydides, notes that Pericles **put to sea from Pegae**, the port of Megara at the eastern end of the Gulf. As Gomme remarks, Plutarch 'throughout exaggerates the success of this expedition' (*Commentary* vol. I., p. 325). That Pericles **inspired such fear in the enemy that they took refuge behind their walls at his approach** seems nothing more than a pious fiction.

The chapter ends with a paean to Pericles' abilities as a leader, although once again it seems incredible that **nothing went wrong, even by accident, from beginning to end of the operations**.

Chapter 20

Plutarch is our only surviving authority for Pericles' expedition to the **Black Sea**, usually dated between 437 and 435. Its aims were, as Plutarch notes, both substantive (Athenian co-settlers at **Sinope**, about midway along the south shore, and at other places like Amisos, which was renamed 'Peiraeus', some 90 miles to the east) and symbolic. Local dynasts like **Timesilaus**, tyrant of Sinope, and Teres, king of the Odrysae in Thrace, were given notice that Athens would not brook any interference with her own interests, which were mainly commercial, the safeguarding of important sources of raw materials, such as wood for shipbuilding, fish and other foodstuffs, and markets for exports of manufactured goods, principally pottery and metal-work.

Lamachus, Pericles' fellow-general on this occasion, served as a type of the preening but somewhat moronic militarist in several of Aristophanes' plays, principally *Archarnians* (425 B.C.). But he showed himself an energetic and intelligent colleague of Nicias and

Alcibiades in the Sicilian campaign, where he fell fighting (414 B.C.). The expedition to the Black Sea was not an unqualified success, for a fragmentary casualty-list (*I. G.* i^2 944) mentions a death at Sinope.

Plutarch shows Pericles applying the curb as well as the goad. That he **refused to be swept along** when certain Athenians (unnamed) **talked of recovering Egypt** may be nothing more than an inference from Thucydides' picture of Pericles as a responsible and even cautious imperialist who, when danger of war threatened, admonished the Athenians 'not to add to the empire while the war is in progress, and not to go out of your way to involve yourselves in new perils' (1.144.1, trans. R. Warner; cf. 2.65.7). If Pericles actually did take the position on Egypt that Plutarch reports, it would be of interest, for no other account of Athens' disastrous involvement there between 459 and 454 B.C. gives any indication of Pericles' attitude to the original undertaking.

It is not clear what basis in fact there is to Plutarch's statement that some Athenians had imperialistic designs on western Greece (**Sicily . . . Carthage and Etruria**) **even as early as this**. We should probably distinguish the areas here named. There is some — not very substantial — evidence for treaties concluded by Athens with Leontini in Sicily and Rhegium in S. Italy in the 440's, which were renewed just before the outbreak of the Peloponnesian War. In the summer of 427 a small Athenian fleet was sent, ostensibly to aid the people of Leontini in their struggle against Syracuse, but actually, Thucydides reports, 'to make a preliminary survey to see whether it would be possible for [the Athenians] to gain control of Sicily' (3.86.4, trans. R. Warner). The real champion of western expansion, however, was **Alcibiades** for whom, according to Plutarch in his *Life of Alcibiades* (chap. 17), Sicily was just a beginning; 'he was dreaming of Carthage and Libya.' Thucydides has him say at Sparta, where he was in exile in the winter of 415, 'Our purpose in sailing against Sicily was to master them first, and after them the Italians, and then to make trial of the Carthaginian empire' (6.90.1; cf. 6.15.2). The report here that **there were even some who dreamed of attacking . . . Etruria** is interesting, if true. Close commercial contacts existed from the 7th century, the Etruscans providing an export market for Greek pottery and other manufactured goods and supplying Athens with raw materials, especially iron ore. An Athenian foothold in Italy was apparently to be guaranteed by the colony at Thurii (see above, chap. 11) and there is some evidence for the involvement of an Athenian naval contingent in a local squabble at Naples, possibly in the 430's.

Chapter 21

The view that Pericles **constantly strove to curb [the Athenians']
extravagant spirit of conquest** is taken directly from Thucydides, who
does, indeed, picture him urging his countrymen (as Plutarch puts it)
**to devote Athens' main strength to guarding and consolidating what
she had already won.** But Thucydides has Pericles taking a stance of
single-minded opposition to Sparta only later, in the mid 430's, when
it was clear that Sparta and her allies would not tolerate Athenian
expansion much longer, and a showdown between the two super-
powers must have appeared to everyone inevitable. It is not clear that
Pericles was giving this advice as early as c. 448 B.C., the date of the
Sacred War described here ('sacred' because it involved Apollo's
holy shrine at **Delphi**).

Sparta even before this had intervened in affairs in north-central
Greece, again adopting a policy in opposition to the **Phocians**; this
was some ten years earlier, c. 457 B.C. Now she tried to counter their
claims to being 'in charge' of the shrine — and so its beneficiaries in
terms of prestige and the wealthy offerings that came into Delphi
from all over the Mediterranean. The Phocians almost inevitably
found the Athenians on their side (in fact, they are described by
Thucydides [1.111.1] as 'allies' of Athens in a campaign in Thessaly
already in about 453 B.C.) and a fragmentary inscription survives —
unfortunately of uncertain date — which does seem to confirm such an
alliance.

Plutarch's main source for this 'Sacred War' is Thucydides
(1.112.5), save for the detail about the inscription on the forehead of
the bronze wolf in the sanctuary. Plutarch had himself probably seen
the statue, which is also mentioned by Pausanias (10.14.7).

Chapter 22

Pericles' decisive and energetic response to the potentially disastrous
double revolt of **Euboea** and **Megara** in 446 B.C. is also narrated at
length by Thucydides (1.114), who in a different place (2.21.1) and
without naming Pericles mentions the story about the bribe. **Pleisto-
anax's** fine, according to Ephorus (*FGH* 70 F 118), was 15 talents,
and his adviser, **Cleandridas**, is reported by Diodorus (13.106.10) —
who may also be drawing on Ephorus, but who gives the name
wrongly as 'Clearchos' — to have spent his exile at Thurii (see chap. 11
above; it did not receive its name until its foundation, several years
after the events described here).

The conviction and banishment is referred to also at *Life of
Lysander* chap. 16 (which Plutarch mentions here) and *Life of Nicias*
chap. 28.

Chapter 23

The earliest allusion to the story of Pericles' remark, **ten talents for 'necessary expenses'**, is in Aristophanes' *Clouds* (v. 859; 423 B.C.). Later writers could not resist embellishing it. Ephorus made the amount twenty talents, and **Theophrastus**, whom Plutarch names here, spun the fantasy that it was a yearly payment by which Pericles **conciliated all the leading men in office** in Sparta.

At the end of the chapter Plutarch returns to Pericles' quelling of the **revolt in Euboea**. To the account in Thucydides (1.114.3) Plutarch adds certain items, such as the figures of **fifty warships and 5,000 hoplites**, and Pericles' alleged motive, seeking reprisals from the people of **Hestiaea** for having **captured an Athenian ship and put the whole crew to death**. It is not known from which of his sources these are taken; Stesimbrotus, Ephorus, Theopompus, Philochorus are all possibilities.

Aristophanes may be hinting at Pericles' ruthlessness, or his quick decisiveness, at any rate, when he has a character in *Clouds* remark, on looking at a map showing Euboea 'stretching out a long way from Athens', that the island had been 'laid out flat by us and Pericles' (vv. 211-13).

Chapter 24

This and the following four chapters constitute the longest single continuous narrative sequence in the *Life*. It is no accident that Thucydides' spare account of the period between the Persian and Peloponnesian Wars here broadens out into something much more leisurely and detailed. Plutarch has the good sense to follow Thucydides very closely, with a sprinkling of personal or minor details from other sources: for Aspasia, the philosophers Plato and Aeschines the Socratic, and the comic writers Cratinus, Eupolis and others unnamed; for the war narrative, Stesimbrotus, Ephorus, Aristotle (probably the *Constitution of the Samians*), Heracleides of Pontus, the Samian Duris and for one detail, Aristophanes.

Samos was a 'charter member' of the Delian Alliance and, along with Chios and Miletus, a valuable and formidable naval power. Pericles was quick to see the danger to the unity of the Alliance (by now really an 'empire') if the rebellion at Samos were not brought decisively under control, and he took forceful measures. Even so, the rebellion covered two campaigning seasons (440 and 439 B.C.), required mobilization of allied naval contingents as well as Athens' (Thucydides mentions ships from Chios and Lesbos), and cost in excess of 1,200 talents. It is amazing that Sparta and her allies did not try to take advantage of the situation; in fact, as Thucydides reports

(1.40.5), intervention was proposed, but Sparta's most powerful associates, the Corinthians, threw their weight against it. Athens was left a free hand in dealing with the recalcitrant Samians.

Plutarch characteristically strays from the main line of his narrative to consider the personal matter of the pressure allegedly brought to bear upon Pericles by his mistress, Aspasia. In chap. 30 below he cites some well-known verses from Aristophanes naming her as (indirectly, at least) the cause of the Peloponnesian War, and it seems probable that another comic writer, Cratinus, made her responsible for the war with Samos in his lost mythological fantasy *Dionysalexandros*. It is possible that these jokes were taken seriously, or even that gossip was mischievously retailed as fact by writers like Duris, who were known to Plutarch but are no longer extant. The comparison of Aspasia with the notorious Milesian courtesan of an earlier age, **Thargelia**, who was for many years the mistress of a powerful Thessalian prince, Antiochus of Pharsalos, is unlikely to be original with Plutarch. Possibly it was first made by Aeschines the Socratic (mentioned by Plutarch in this chapter) in his dialogue *Aspasia*.

When Plutarch returns from Aspasia's alleged model, Thargelia, to Aspasia herself, he transmits as sober if not very edifying fact what almost certainly originated as satirical overstatement, both on the comic stage and among the writers who admired and wrote about Socrates. All the items which Plutarch records are suspect:

(1) What attracted Pericles to Aspasia was not her good looks and physical appeal but **her rare political wisdom**. This is precisely the joke made by Plato in the *Menexenos* (cited by Plutarch later in the chapter), where she is the author of the peculiar 'Funeral Speech' reported by Socrates in the dialogue, and alleged to be the ghost-writer of the famous funeral oration delivered by Pericles after the first year of the Peloponnesian War (*Menex.* 235e).

(2) **Socrates visited her from time to time with his disciples**. This is the assumption put forward by Plato in the *Menexenos*, and another follower of Socrates, Xenophon, twice has Socrates defer to Aspasia for her superior wisdom in some matter (*Memorabilia* 2.6.36; *Oeconomicus* 3.14). The extent to which this kind of silliness could be carried is illustrated by some verses purported to have been composed by Aspasia in which she advised Socrates to assuage his desire for Alcibiades by sending him love-poetry, 'bridal gifts for his soul', that is, endearments which would induce Alcibiades to unveil his true self like a new bride (Athenaeus 5.219 B-C quoting the second-century B.C. writer Herodicus).

(3) **Some of his close friends brought their wives to listen to her conversation**. Aeschines the Socratic, whom Plutarch names in this chapter in another connection, is cited for the story of Xenophon and his wife attending a logical disquisition by Aspasia (Cicero, *On*

Invention 1.31.51). Why the Socratic circle chose to paint this faintly ridiculous and almost certainly untrue picture of Pericles' mistress it is only possible to guess. It is part of the same debunking of fifth-century politicians as we find in Plato's *Gorgias*, only now satire has been taken over by later writers as fact.

Even Plutarch's statements regarding **Lysicles the sheep-dealer** are not above suspicion. What is certainly known about him, beyond his relationship with Aspasia after Pericles' death, is that he survived Pericles by little more than a year and that, as general in charge of a special revenue-collecting mission in the eastern Mediterranean, he fell in battle against the Carians near the Maeander river in 428 B.C. (Thucydides 3.19.2). This would hardly have given Aspasia sufficient time to work the transformation that—once more on the authority of Aeschines—she is alleged to have wrought: 'she rigged Lysicles out as a very skilled orator, just as she had prepared Pericles to be a demagogue' (Scholiast on the *Menexenus* passage cited above). It is even possible that the reference to him as a 'sheep- dealer' or 'sheep-seller' rests on a misunderstood joke in Aristophanes. In a comic sequence in *Knights*, produced in 424 B.C., there is a satirical catalogue of political leaders designated as 'sellers of so-and-so' (vv. 128ff.). Third in succession is the 'leather-seller Paphlagon', who is taken to represent the demagogue Cleon (see chaps. 33 and 35 below). But the fourth, a 'Sausage-seller', who is destined to supplant Cleon, is clearly fictitious, and so may be the first two, a 'Hemp-seller' and a 'Sheep- seller', whom the ancient commentators were anxious to identify as real individuals, Eucrates (about whom nothing is known) and 'Callias or, according to some, Lysicles the sheep-seller'. Since the comedians regularly called the Athenian electorate 'sheep', and so easily deceived (cf. *Wasps* 955), Aristophanes may have used 'sheep-seller' to denote any glib political orator rather than a real individual.

A serious disagreement exists between Plutarch and some modern authorities about the exact sequence of Pericles' marriage and his **attachment to Aspasia**. Plutarch says unequivocally that Pericles' wife, whose name is nowhere recorded in the sources and about whom very little is known beyond the information given here, **was closely related to** him and **had been married first of all to Hipponicus**. J.K. Davies calls this statement of Plutarch's 'certainly mistaken' (*Athenian Properties Families* [Oxford, 1971] p. 262). Davies bases his argument on calculations of the respective ages of the two sets of children whom the lady bore to her two husbands. He contends that genealogical considerations show that Pericles' two legitimate sons, **Xanthippus and Paralus**, who died in the Great Plague of 430 B.C. (see chap. 36 below), were older than the lady's two other children by **Hipponicus** (one of whom was the Callias mentioned by the Scholiast on *Knights* 132, noted just above). The reasoning, however, is complex and the evidence anything but straightforward, and some recent accounts accept Plutarch's unique testimony (see, e.g., the first article by Cromey mentioned in the Bibliography to Endnote F below). In fact, Plutarch is usually both well-informed and careful to get his facts right on matters of genealogy of this kind (see, e.g., *Themistocles* chap. 32, *Aristeides* chap. 27).

The story that Pericles, on leaving for the agora or returning home, **greeted [Aspasia] with a kiss**, looks like a variant upon, or may even be derived from, the statement quoted by Athenaeus (13.589e) from Antisthenes the philosopher (see Intro., sec. 3), that he left home and returned twice a day just to be able to kiss her more often. In any case, a pun is being perpetrated on her name which etymologically ought to mean 'Loved' or 'Kissable'.

Plutarch returns to one of his favourite sources of information in this *Life*, allusions in the comic poets. **Omphale** and **Deianeira** were, respectively, the Lydian mistress and the longsuffering wife of Heracles, who must, therefore, have allegorically represented Pericles in these comedies. There was a satyr-drama *Omphale* by Ion of Chios (see chaps. 5 above and 28 below), but there is nothing in the 18 or so fragmentary verses or phrases cited from it to show that it was a political satire. (A reference to Aspasia as Omphale by Cratinus has been found in the much-emended scholion to Plato's *Menexenos*, already mentioned.) There may be an extra, malicious point in calling Aspasia 'Omphale' since the myths had Heracles in bondage to and even exchanging clothes with the imperious queen.

With Aspasia-Hera we are back to the comic allusions of chap. 3 above, which made Pericles out to be Zeus. The lines from **Cratinus** (fr. 259 Kassel-Austin), although similar in intent to the passage from the same poet's *Cheirons* cited in chap. 3, are much coarser, 'Vice' being the translator's pale rendering of the Greek word, which literally means 'Buggery'. Although none of these lost plays can be dated with any assurance, these attacks on Pericles seem so violent, even vicious, that some scholars believe that Pericles reacted by causing to be passed a piece of legislation referred to as a 'gag-law on comedy'. It is reported by one source (a scholion on Aristophanes, *Acharnians* 67; Fornara 111) to have remained in effect for over two years, from 440 to 438 B.C. Since a total prohibition of comic performances seems unlikely, it may have restricted only the kind of personal vilification recorded by Plutarch here. As Gomme remarks in his *Commentary on Thucydides* (vol. I, p. 387) this 'would be of great interest if we knew more about it'.

Plutarch had already quoted a line from **Eupolis'** famous play, *The Demes*, in chap. 3 above. The scene he alludes to here must have formed a dramatic climax, when Pericles, the last hero to be conjured from Hades along with other generals from by-gone days of Athens' military glory, including **Myronides** (see chap. 16 above), asks the latter about his 'bastard son' (the translation omits 'bastard'), Pericles the younger. Myronides replies that what is preventing the lad from becoming a 'real man' is the ignominy of his birth. The translation 'citizen' is slightly misleading; as the account in chap. 37 below makes clear, Pericles asked for—and presumably obtained—a grant of citizenship for the boy before his death. Eupolis' joke probably involves an imputation of cowardice in a public command some time before the date of production, c. 412 B.C. (It was in *The Demes* that there occurred the famous lines about Pericles' oratorical ability; see Intro., sec. 3).

The chapter ends as it began, with Aspasia compared to another famous royal concubine, **Milto** of Phocaea. The source of this story of the name-change is identified by Athenaeus (13, 576d) as 'Zeno-phanes', whose date is uncertain. Plutarch's comment that the **details concerning Aspasia come into my mind as I write** throws interesting light, as Gomme remarks, on his method of composition, especially his reliance on what must have been prodigious powers of memory.

Chapter 25

The continuous narrative in this and the subsequent three chapters is based principally on Thucydides (1.115.2-117), from whom fully 90% of the factual material is drawn. Other minor details derive probably from authorities named in chap. 28. Of these the most important was Ephorus, named also in chap. 27, who, as most scholars believe, was used extensively by Diodorus in his narrative of the Samian War (12.27-28). Even Diodorus' account, however, as Gomme remarks (*Commentary on Thucydides*, vol. I, p. 355) is largely dependent on Thucydides, as, for example, in the numbers of ships involved.

The war between Samos and Miletus broke out **over the possession of Priene**, which was 'north of Miletos, near Mykale, and so not only lay between Miletos and Samos, but bordered on the Samian territory on the mainland' (Gomme).

Plutarch agrees with Thucydides (1.115.3) about the number of hostages, but Thucydides has no reference to each being **ready to give Pericles a talent**. This may be a variation of the story in Diodorus (12.27.2) that Pericles both took 80 boys as hostages *and* exacted 80 talents as a fine. Again, although the whole account regarding **Pissuthnes, the Persian satrap** (provincial governor) of Sardis is Thucydidean, there is no report there that he **sent Pericles 10,000 gold staters** (a standard coin in the eastern Mediterranean).

Pericles' decision to **set up a democracy** to replace the previous aristocratic government, now in rebellion against Athens, fits the standard pattern. The same thing had happened some ten years previously at Miletus, the other belligerent in this war. The Athenians no doubt preferred to deal with democratically elected governments like their own, but they were not doctrinaire in the matter.

That the Samians **were defiantly resolved to fight the Athenians for the mastery of the seas** is Plutarch's own inference, probably on the basis of a remark made by Thucydides in another place, which is cited at the end of chap. 28 below. Details of the **naval battle near an island called Tragia** and the precise numbers and type of ships are taken straight from Thucydides.

Chapter 26

Plutarch follows Diodorus (12.27.4)—or their common source, Ephorus—for the detail that Pericles went off **to intercept a fleet of Phoenician ships**. Thucydides says, more cautiously, 'news had arrived that the Phoenician fleet was on its way' (1.116.3), and this, as Gomme notes, is the likelier version. Plutarch rightly rejects **Stesimbrotus'** tale (*FGH* 107 F 8) that Pericles' **intention was to attack Cyprus**. Aristotle (probably in the *Constitution of the Samians*) may have been Plutarch's source for the name of the Samian commander, **Melissus**, but the additional item for which Aristotle is cited, that **Pericles himself was defeated by Melissus in an earlier sea-battle** (fr. 535 Rose), is incorrect. It rests on a confusion between the two battles, from the first of which, as Thucydides and Plutarch make clear, Pericles was absent.

Melissus, who is also mentioned by Plutarch in *The Life of Themistocles* (chap. 2), was a 'natural' philosopher, that is, one who investigated the composition and functioning of the material world. Thus he was in the long tradition of Ionian philosophers, some of whom were natives of Miletus, who specialized in this kind of theorizing. The later biographical tradition was impressed by the fact that he combined the life of the mind with his career as a naval commander, a position in which, as Diogenes Laertius reports (9.24), he 'was even more admired because of his own proper merit'. What also occasioned comment was the unusual situation that in this war a philosopher was pitted against a dramatist, for, as was noted above (chap. 8), the poet Sophocles was elected as one of the ten generals in the first part of the war.

Plutarch's version of the branding story is repeated by the ninth-century Byzantine scholar Photios. A variant account had it that the Athenians put their own emblem, the owl, on captured prisoners. Elsewhere, Plutarch reports that the Athenians taken prisoner at Syracuse were branded with a horse (*Life of Nicias* 29). Prof. Sansone remarks that 'there is evidence for the use of coin-dies as brands.' The Athenians could thus have used their coin-dies, which depicted Athena's owl, for this purpose. It is possible that

Aristophanes' early play *Babylonians*, produced in 426 B.C. when the comedian was still in his mid-twenties, allegorically represented the plight of these branded Samians, as scholars have inferred from the excellent pun with which the chapter ends (Aristophanes frag. 71 Kassel-Austin; 'deeply lettered' could also mean 'marked by many signs').

The tyrant **Polycrates** ruled Samos from c. 540 to 522 B.C. and was responsible for turning the island into a major sea-power in the Mediterranean. He did this mainly by maintaining a large fleet (Herodotus [3.39] mentions 100 penteconters or 50-oared vessels), by constructing a sheltered, defensible harbour (Herodotus 3.60), and by being willing to innovate in the matter of ship-design, as illustrated by Plutarch's comments here, which may have been a kind of proto-trireme, with two instead of three banks of oars.

Chapter 27

Plutarch is embellishing Thucydides' narrative when he gives, as Pericles' reason for laying siege to the city, that he preferred the expenditure **of time and money rather than of the wounds and the lives of his fellow citizens**. This fits the picture we are given in this section of the *Life* of a general cautious almost to a fault, always with his troops' safety uppermost in his mind. Compare the comment recorded at the end of chap. 38 below.

Plutarch has remembered some previous writer's rather peculiar explanation of the saying, 'a white day'. The ultimate source is probably not Ephorus, who will be named shortly below, since the story is not found in Diodorus; nor Duris, whose account was distinctly anti-Periclean. **Heracleides of Pontus** (fr. 60 Wehrli) is cited for his rebuttal of **Ephorus**' identification (*FGH* 70 F 194) of **Artemon the engineer**. He cannot have been the **Artemon Periphoretus** ('carried about in a little hammock') who is mockingly described by **Anacreon** (frs. 372 and 388 Page, *Poetae Melici Graeci*), for the obvious chronological reason that that Artemon would have lived at least 60 years too early. Perhaps Ephorus was misled by a joke in a play like Eupolis' *Flatterers*, in which the Samian siege was alluded to (fr. 154 Edmonds). A butt of one of Aristophanes' jokes is called 'Artemon Periponeros', 'scoundrelly' (*Acharnians* 850), and there is a reference to 'new'—metaphorical—'siege-engines' at *Clouds* 479-80.

The description which Plutarch gives of his **luxurious habits** applies to the earlier not the later Artemon. Quite apart from the confusion over Artemon, suspicion adheres to the whole story of the siege-engines, which Gomme calls 'almost certainly false' (*Commentary on Thuc.* vol. I, p. 354).

Chapter 28

The bare facts of the war's conclusion are in Thucydides (1.117.3). Diodorus (12.28.3) gives the amount of the **heavy fine** as 200 talents, a figure generally emended to '1,200'. Plutarch criticizes **Duris the Samian** (see Intro., sec. 3 and R.B. Kebric, *In the Shadow of Macedon: Duris of Samos* [*Historia Einzelschriften* no. 29; Wiesbaden, 1977] pp. 15ff.) for his tendency to **magnify these events into a tragedy**. (For Plutarch's use of expressions of this kind, see P. de Lacy, 'Biography as Tragedy in Plutarch', *American Journal of Philology* 73 [1952] 159-71.) As Plutarch notes, Duris' **personal interests** made it almost inevitable that he should have **blacken[ed] the name of Athens**. **Aristotle's** *Constitution of the Samians*, which was probably one of Plutarch's sources, contained the detail that after their defeat the Samians had to grant 'isopolity' (equality of civic rights) to their slaves (fr. 575 Rose).

Pericles was chosen to honour those **who had lost their lives in the campaign** by declaiming **the speech . . . over their tombs**, as he was to do later after the first year of the war with Sparta. Several memorable phrases from it found their way into the tradition, the one reported by Plutarch in chap. 8 above, from Stesimbrotus, and the striking simile that 'the removal from the city of her young men was as if the spring had been taken out of the year,' mentioned twice by Aristotle in the *Rhetoric* (see Intro., sec. 3).

The exchange between Pericles and Cimon's sister, **Elpinice**, may or may not be true; suspicions are stirred by the somewhat similar anecdote in chap. 10. In any case, her point is well taken: Pericles had marshalled Athens' energies **not in a war against the Persians or the Phoenicians . . . but in destroying a Greek city**, and a staunch ally at that. All Pericles could do was retort unchivalrously by citing the verse that **Archilochus** had probably aimed at an elderly prostitute (fr. 205 West). Elpinice was by now at least 65, since elsewhere Plutarch describes her as 'a young girl and unmarried' in 489 B.C. (*Cimon* chap. 4).

The story from **Ion** of Chios (*FGH* 392 F 16) perhaps comes from his book *Sojourns*. His charge of arrogance against Pericles had already been cited in chap. 5 above. As Gomme observed, 'Ion did not like Perikles' (*Commentary on Thucydides* vol. I, p. 358).

Chapter 29

Plutarch continues with his essentially Thucydidean account. After an interval of six years, in the summer of 433 B.C., **Pericles persuaded the Athenians to send help to Corcyra** (modern Corfu), a colony of but now also at **war with Corinth**. Longstanding animosity between the two cities had erupted into war over control of a joint colony, Epidamnus (modern Durazzo in Albania). Although by terms of the so-called 'Thirty Years' Peace', concluded between Athens and Sparta in 445 B.C. (to which Plutarch is probably referring by the phrase **articles of peace entered into upon oath** later in the chapter) Corcyra was technically free to join the Athenian alliance, such an action was bound to be taken as unfriendly by the Corinthians. They then applied considerable pressure on Sparta to check Athens' growing power in Greece once and for all.

No doubt one of Pericles' motives in urging the alliance with Corcyra was, as Plutarch says, her **powerful navy**, which Thucydides numbers at 120, but these turned out not to be of much help to Athens in the war with Sparta.

Thucydides (1.45.2) names the three generals sent by Athens, among them **Lacedaemonius, the son of Cimon**; financial and other details concerning the expedition are also recorded in an inscription, which survives (M.N. Tod, *A Selection of Greek Historical Inscriptions* [2nd. ed., Oxford, 1946] no. 55). It is true that the original squadron of 10 ships was too small to do much good, and Pericles was almost certainly criticized for it. What is not clear is that there are grounds to the personal motive ascribed, that Pericles was out **to humiliate** Lacedaemonius, 'who had been hipparch [cavalry officer] c. 446 B.C. and with two others had dedicated an equestrian statue on the Acropolis from enemy spoils' (Gomme, *Commentary on Thucydides* vol. I, p. 177). It is possible that the Athenians wished to avoid getting too deeply involved in a military confrontation with Corinth, and that the ten ships represent a half-hearted response, or a bit of 'fence-sitting', such as was contemplated at the time of the Sicilian campaign in 415. In any case, these were **reinforced . . . later with a larger squadron**, twenty ships according to Thucydides (1.50.5).

Plutarch's source for Pericles' animus against Cimon's sons was Stesimbrotus (*FGH* 107 F 6), who is cited for an identical account at *Life of Cimon* chap. 16. The names he gave his sons reflect, as Plutarch states, Cimon's pro-Spartan leanings as well as a wider international outlook.

Thucydides is Plutarch's main, although not his only, source for the international events which led up to the Peloponnesian War, the grievances and complaints laid by some of Sparta's allies against Athens, and the pressure thus brought to bear upon the rather reluctant Spartans to declare war. The Megarian complaint about **being shut out and driven away from every market and every harbour which the Athenians controlled** (the so-called 'Megarian Decree', which Plutarch will return to in chap. 30; see Endnote D) is passed over by Thucydides very lightly (1.67.4, 1.139.1). Likewise the **grievances** of the **people of Aegina**, who, according to Thucydides

(1.67.2; 1.140.3), charged that they were not allowed to be 'autonomous' according to the terms of the Thirty Years' Peace. Scholars disagree over what such autonomy might have consisted in, given that Aegina (the 'eye-sore of the Peiraeus', as Pericles had termed it, chap. 8 above) had been defeated in battle c. 457 B.C., forced to take down her fortifications and hand over her fleet—the treatment later meted out to Samos—and assessed a fairly stiff annual tribute (Thucydides 1.108.4).

Thucydides gives a much more detailed account of the Corcyraean and Potidaean affairs (1.24-55, and 1.56-65 respectively). Plutarch's brief reference to the latter brings out but does not underline the ambiguous legal position of **Potidaea** which was both a **colony of Corinth** and **subject to Athens**, that is, a tribute-paying member of the Delian Confederacy. As Thucydides reports, Athens decided on a pre-emptive use of force and, even before any open revolt on Potidaea's part, insisted that she dismantle her fortifications, send hostages to Athens and expel the magistrates sent annually from Corinth as mother-city (1.56.2). Though the underdog, Potidaea's hands were not entirely clean, for she was negotiating with both sides, asking Athens for leniency and Sparta for armed support if necessary (1.58.)

The really valuable contribution made by Plutarch to our knowledge of these preliminaries to war is contained in the number of circumstantial details he records concerning Athens' treatment of Megara and the personal attacks made on Pericles at this time. These topics take up the remainder of this and the following three chapters, and on both of them Thucydides is extremely reticent, so that Plutarch's discursiveness is all the more welcome.

Thucydides praises **Archidamus, the Spartan king** (for whom see chap. 8 above), as one who was 'both shrewd'—a rare quality in a Spartan—'and moderate' (1.79.2), and reports a speech of his in which he **strove to placate his allies and bring about a peaceful settlement of most of their grievances** (1.80-85).

Chapter 30

Plutarch's additions to Thucydides' account (1.139) of negotiations over the **Megarian decree** are circumstantial, even anecdotal, but not necessarily therefore fictitious or untrue. He names one of the Spartan **envoys, Polyalces**, and tells what Gomme calls a 'pretty story' of verbal badinage between this man and Pericles (*Commentary on Thucydides*, vol. I., p. 449). Did Plutarch himself infer the possibility that Pericles may have **harboured some private grudge against the Megarians**, perhaps with nothing more solid to go on than the passage from Aristophanes' *Acharnians* which he cites at the end of the chapter? Or did he find it in one of his sources, e.g. Ephorus, who was perhaps himself only guessing? We cannot be certain, but, even if only a conjecture, it is a suggestion that should be taken seriously. The charge that they had **appropriated for their own profane use the territory of Eleusis** is essentially that recorded by Thucydides, who, however, adds a further charge, that they had harboured slaves who had escaped from Athens (1.139.2).

Plutarch appears to be well-informed about the stages by which hostilities escalated, and he names specific individuals involved, the **herald who was sent** to lodge the original complaint, **Anthemocritus**, and the mover of the punitive **decree against them, Charinus**. Nothing further is known about either man, although in one of his Essays (*Moralia* 812 D) Plutarch lists Charinus as an agent of Pericles, along with Menippus (see above chap. 13), Ephialtes and Lampon. This is a mere inference, and gives us no new facts beyond the information in the present chapter, that he moved the decree. For the general credibility of Plutarch's account, see Endnote D.

The invasion of **the Megarid twice in each year** is confirmed by Thucydides (4.66.1). The first was led by Pericles himself, with the whole Athenian army including metics, in the autumn of 431 (2.31.1). The practice was discontinued in 424 B.C. (2.31.3).

The **Thriasian** or **Dipylon** Gate, where Anthemocritus was buried, was situated at the northwest corner of the fortification wall. There the roads converged which connected Athens with Peiraeus, Eleusis and the Thriasian plain (hence the name). Just outside was the outer Cerameicus, which Thucydides calls 'the city's most beautiful suburb' (2.34.5) and it was here that Athens' war-dead were given solemn public burial.

It is hard to believe Plutarch's assertion that the **Megarians . . . threw the blame for the Athenians' actions upon Pericles** by quoting verses 524-27 of **Aristophanes' 'Acharnians'**, which was produced in 424 B.C. It seems likelier that some historian, probably Ephorus, was misled by this comic 'explanation' of the war invented by Aristophanes. Similarly, Aristophanes' alternative but equally ludicrous account of the cause of the war, that in an effort to save Pheidias from prosecution Pericles 'threw in a small spark, the Megarian Decree, and fanned up so large a war that all the Greeks' eyes smarted from the smoke' (*Peace* 609-11), was accepted as sober history by Ephorus (*FGH* 70 F 196 = Diodorus 12.40-41) and ultimately found its way into Plutarch's pages (end of chap. 32 below).

As an example of the patently absurd conclusion drawn by careless or incompetent writers who took seriously some of these jokes in comedy I note a passage in Athenaeus, an Egyptian anthologist writing about A.D. 200. He quotes the lines cited by Plutarch from **Acharnians** and comments: 'Aspasia imported into Greece a throng of beautiful women and the whole of Greece was filled with her prostitutes' (13.569 F).

Chapter 31

Plutarch concludes his discussion of the Megarian Decree with a remark with which few would disagree, that the real cause or origin of the decree (he uses the semi-technical word '*archê*') is **extremely hard to discover**. He then offers contrasting explanations, one favourable, the other unfavourable to Pericles. The former is Thucydides', who has Pericles say: 'Let none of you think that we are going to war for a small matter . . . For this 'small' matter involves the entire confirmation and test of your resolve. If you give in to them on this, they will soon have others, more significant orders to give you, since you submitted on this through fear' (1.140.4-5).

Pericles' special relationship with the sculptor **Pheidias** had already been mentioned (chap. 13 above), as well as the silly story that Pheidias had used his art-works to lure women for Pericles' pleasures. Now Plutarch returns to what he terms **the most damning charge of all**—in fact, two charges, the first the serious one of embezzlement with respect to the gold plates used on the Athena Parthenos statue, the second (which strikes us as frivolous, although the Athenians took this kind of thing quite seriously) a charge presumably of impiety for allegedly incorporating portrait-likenesses of himself and Pericles among the figures sculpted on Athena's shield. As was mentioned above in the note to chap. 30, the joke in Aristophanes' *Peace* 605ff. (produced in 421 B.C.) only makes comic sense if Pheidias did get into some kind of trouble: Aristophanes' character says, 'Pheidias began the ruin of peace because of the fix he got in' (vv. 604-5). As far as we can judge, it was Ephorus (= Diodorus) who spelled this out as a charge of embezzlement brought by one or more of Pheidias' assistants (Diodorus 12.39.1 uses the plural but gives no names; Plutarch here names only a certain **Menon**, about whom nothing further is known). If we accept that such a trial took place, we should leave it where Diodorus and Plutarch date it, just before the outbreak of the war, in spite of the doubts cast upon the chronology by the writer of Athenian local history, Philochorus (see Intro., sec. 3), who apparently placed Pheidias' condemnation and escape from Athens six years earlier, in 438/7 (*FGH* 328F 121, from a Scholiast on *Peace* 605, where, however, the archon-years are garbled and have had to be extensively emended).

The sources are probably correct to say that what really made Pheidias vulnerable was **his friendship with Pericles**. It is even possible that a separate or joint accusation was laid against Pericles himself as official 'overseer' of the Parthenon project. Diodorus hints darkly at 'accusations and slanders' against him (12.39.2), and Plutarch gives in chap. 32 below what appear to be circumstantial details of full legal proceedings. What should be treated with utmost suspicion, however, is Plutarch's statement that Pheidias was acquitted by having the **gold used for the statue . . . taken off and weighed**. Thucydides does, indeed, comment that 'the gold to the weight of 40 talents could all be removed' (2.13.5), and it looks as if a later writer—perhaps a comic dramatist—could not resist making a juicy story of it: not only had Pericles designed it that way (as Plutarch says) **from the very beginning**, it also came in useful when his friend Pheidias was on trial! (Plutarch gives a more credible motive at *Moralia* 828 B: so that the gold could be removed and used for the expenses of the war, which is also the implication of Thuc. 2.13.5.)

The statue itself was a masterpiece of luxurious good taste. The following is Pausanias' description. 'The statue is made of ivory and gold [that is, ivory for the flesh parts and gold for the cloak and other accoutrements] . . . Athene stands upright in an ankle-length tunic with the head of Medusa carved in ivory on her breast. She has [in her hand] a Victory about eight feet high, and a spear in her hand and a shield at her feet, and a snake beside the shield . . . The plinth of the statue is carved with the birth of Pandora.' (1.24.5 and 7, trans. P. Levi).

The second charge, that Pheidias glorified himself and his patron through likenesses on the shield, is probably just malicious gossip. Holden in his note on this passage in Plutarch draws attention to the fact that on the so-called Strangford shield (based on a Roman copy of Pheidias' original sculpture) there are 'two figures which exactly tally with Plutarch's description'. It seems easier to believe that the story was invented to fit these two figures rather than the reverse. (Pausanias [5.11.4] recounts a similar story, that Pheidias put a picture of a boyfriend of his from Elis on one of the bars of the throne of his Zeus statue at Olympia; in another version, he wrote the boy's name on Zeus' finger. The same kind of accusations were made against the painter Polygnotus. Presumably ancient artists got used to this kind of racy gossip.) On the other hand, the choice of theme itself may have been intended to glorify Pericles, at least in general terms. The invasion of Athens by the warlike women known as *Amazons* had become a popular tale; it was referred to by Athena herself in Aeschylus' *Eumenides* (vv. 685ff.; produced 458 B.C.) and had been depicted on one of the Parthenon's north metopes. Athens' enlightened and heroic king, Theseus, had driven them off. What better story to represent allegorically the superiority of Athenian civilization to barbarism, especially under the inspired guidance of her modern Theseus, Pericles.

The version of Pheidias' end reported here, that he **was cast into prison and there he fell sick and died**, is probably Ephorus', although it is not found in Diodorus. Philochorus (see above) had a different story: he escaped to Elis some years previously, received a commission to execute the colossal seated Zeus mentioned above in chap. 2, and was there put to death (presumably on a similar charge of embezzlement). (See Gomme vol. II, pp. 184ff., esp. 186; Fornara 116)

Whatever official document, whether genuine or forged, that Plutarch's source cited named **Glycon** as proposer of a decree heaping various honours upon Pheidias' accuser, **Menon**. As Gomme notes (*Commentary on Thucydides* vol. II, p. 185 n.1) the grant of exemption **from all taxes** goes beyond the inducements promised to the informer that are mentioned earlier in the chapter; Gomme says he is 'doubtful about this'.

Chapter 32

Plutarch narrates further assaults on Pericles through his friends. The story of Aspasia's **trial for impiety** contains several suspicious features. First, although it is not impossible that she was literally **prosecuted by Hermippus the comic poet** (some lines of his are cited in chap. 33 below), it is equally possible, as some scholars have maintained, that the story originated in a satirical scene from one of his plays. Our confidence is not increased by the charge allegedly brought, **procuring free-born Athenian women for Pericles and receiving them into her house**. This sounds like a doublet of the equally dubious accusations against Pheidias and his art-work, and Pyrilampes and his peacocks, in chap. 13 above. The philosopher **Anaxagoras**, whose name Plutarch had introduced repeatedly earlier in the *Life* as Pericles' main mentor (chaps. 4,5,6 and 8), reportedly fell foul of the law because of his connections with the statesman. The credibility of this story is hopelessly entangled in what appear to be insoluble chronological problems (see Endnote E). In any case, Plutarch asks his readers to believe that Pericles intervened directly to save both Aspasia and Anaxagoras from prosecution. Towards the end of the chapter he cites **Aeschines**, a follower of Socrates and writer of dialogue in the style of Plato (see Intro., sec. 3 and chap. 24 above) for the story that **Pericles contrived to beg off Aspasia by bursting into floods of tears during her trial**. (In fact there is some doubt whether Plutarch is correct in naming Aeschines, for Athenaeus [13. 589 E] gives a similar account on the authority of Antisthenes, another student of Socrates; see chap. 24 above for a further detail apparently drawn from Antisthenes.) Now, if Aspasia really was hailed into court, Pericles as her *kurios* (husband or legal 'protector') would certainly have been involved, but if we reject altogether the story of Aspasia's trial, all this is fiction, amusing but rather malicious.

For **Anaxagoras**, the matter is somewhat more complicated. Plutarch says that Pericles **smuggled him out of the city** before he could stand trial (also at *Life of Nicias* chap. 23). But a different, incompatible, account was current of Pericles' involvement in Anaxagoras' trial: Pericles had to defend him in person against a charge of impiety brought by Cleon (named in chaps. 33 and 35 below as an accuser of Pericles himself), but he was found guilty, fined five talents and banished (Diogenes Laertius [2.12] quoting Sotion, who wrote about 200 B.C.; see Intro., sec. 3). The biographical tradition about Anaxagoras points pretty certainly to a trial for atheism, and Plutarch may be drawing on a sound source when he names Anaxagoras' accuser as **Diopeithes the diviner**, whose name is sometimes linked with that of the soothsayer Lampon (mentioned in chap. 6 above) and who was ridiculed by Aristophanes, Telecleides and other comic writers as 'a religious maniac and fanatical dispenser of oracles' (D.M. MacDowell, n. on *Wasps* 380). W.K.C. Guthrie comments on the appropriateness of the name 'Diopeithes', literally, 'he-who-trusts-in-God', for one cast as a defender of traditional beliefs (*The Sophists* [Cambridge, 1971] 228 n. 2). What is not at all clear, however, is whether Anaxagoras' trial formed part of the larger pattern of attacks against Pericles that Plutarch is discussing here, or whether his prosecution really occurred c. 450 B.C. (see Endnote E).

The most serious problem in this chapter is whether Plutarch had any trustworthy authority for the information he reports concerning the apparently separate indictment against Pericles **for embezzlement or bribery or malversation** brought by **Dracontides** and **amended by Hagnon**. Plutarch is our only source for these alleged 'facts' and the very circumstantial nature of his account has made many scholars want to accept it. Dracontides is a name borne by a single individual, or several, who were involved in various public events in this period (see MacDowell's n. on *Wasps* 157). Hagnon was a colleague of Pericles in the Samian campaign as well as leader of colonists to Amphipolis in 437 B.C. (Thucydides 1.117.2 and 4.102.3 respectively). He is, therefore, a likely person to modify the original motion in a way favourable to Pericles, whose treatment would have been more equitable in **a case . . . tried in the usual way** than under the extraordinary procedure suggested by Dracontides. Gomme (*Commentary* vol. II., p. 187) accepted the substance of Plutarch's account — 'both decrees seem clearly to be authentic', he wrote — but argued strenuously against the implied date 432 B.C. He preferred to transfer all these attacks, and the decrees here recorded, to the late summer of 430 B.C., which is the only place that Thucydides (2.59.2-3 and 2.65.3-4) reports any judicial proceedings against

Pericles, the deposition from office which Plutarch records in chap. 35 below, and his reinstatement at chap. 37. To me this seems unsound method. If we are to accept Plutarch's testimony (as I believe we should), his date, too, should be accepted. In that case, Thucydides, for his own reasons, has passed over in silence all these attempts to weaken Pericles' authority on the eve of the war.

Towards the end of the chapter Plutarch comments that as a diversionary tactic, since **the war was threatening and smouldering . . . he deliberately fanned it into flame**. The words are a paraphrase of Aristophanes' joke in Peace 609ff., quoted in the note to chap. 30 above. Plutarch has been misled by the gullible Ephorus.

The chapter closes with an observation with which, given the fragmentary and self-contradictory nature of the sources, it would be hard to disagree: **the true history of these events is hidden from us.**

Chapter 33

Plutarch resumes his narrative of events just before war finally broke out. His source is once again principally (though not solely) Thucydides. Pericles' mother Agariste (see chap. 3 above) was a member of the Alcmaeonidae. An early member of this family, Megacles, had incurred ritual defilement or **blood-guilt** by going back on his promise of religious immunity to a certain Cylon, who had failed in an attempt to set up a tyranny at Athens c. 632 B.C. The story is told in full by **Thucydides** (1.126-127), and with some alteration of detail by Herodotus (5.71), as well as by Plutarch himself elsewhere (*Life of Solon* 12). The 'curse' had been used against Pericles' great-uncle, the lawgiver Cleisthenes, by his political enemies in 5O8 B.C. Now it was Pericles' turn. As Thucydides explains, in making the demand the Spartans didn't really expect the Athenians to expel Pericles (as they had done to Cleisthenes), but simply hoped that his position of pre-eminence would be weakened. That it was not, and that **this manoeuvre produced exactly the opposite effect**, are inferences by Plutarch, but reasonable ones.

Pericles' offer to **present all his lands and the buildings on them to the state** if they were spared by the Spartan king **Archidamus** (see chaps. 8 and 29 above) comes from Thucydides (2.13.1), as does the halt of the invading Spartan army at **Acharnae** (2.2O.4) about 7 miles north of Athens. A similar story was told about Hannibal's sparing of the estates of Fabius Maximus (*Life of Fabius* chap. 7), a parallelism which may have led Plutarch to compare Fabius with Pericles. The people of this region provided a large complement of the Athenian army and had a reputation as good but excitable fighters (hence the appropriateness of Aristophanes' choice in making them the chorus of his comedy in 424 B.C., from which Plutarch cites a passage at the end of chap. 30 above). Thucydides explains that the Spartans thought they would put intolerable pressure on Pericles to march out and risk a land-battle, which would have been disastrous for the Athenians.

It is not known where Plutarch got the figure **60,000 Peloponnesian and Boeotian hoplites**, which he also mentions in the *Moralia* (784 E). As Holden notes, the writer of Athenian history Androtion gives an even higher figure, 100,000.

Plutarch follows Thucydides (2.22.1) for Pericles' refusal to **summon the Assembly**, although it is not clear what powers he was exercising in thus interfering with the normal proceses of the democracy. Perhaps, 'the prestige Pericles enjoyed as a statesman rather than any power vested in him as a general enabled him to prevail on his fellow-generals and the council to postpone all meetings of the people until the immediate danger of the Spartan invasion was over' (C. Hignett, *A History of the Athenian Constitution* [Oxford, 1952] p. 247). Plutarch may be quoting directly Pericles' remark '**trees, even if they are lopped or cut down, can quickly grow again . . .**,' but this is possibly only a reminiscence or paraphrase of Thucydides' version of the address made by Pericles to the Athenians on the eve of the war: 'What we should lament is not the loss of houses or land, but the loss of men's lives: men come first; the rest is the fruit of their labour' (1.143.5, trans. R. Warner).

The picture of Pericles behaving **like the helmsman of a ship** is an expansion of the kind of metaphor Plutarch is fond of (see chap. 15 above, especially the reference to Plato, *Republic* 488 Aff. for the extended 'Ship of State' image). A particularly striking use of nautical imagery in a political context occurs at Aeschylus, *Seven against Thebes* 62ff., of which these may be reminiscences.

To Thucydides' report of the abuse heaped on Pericles for **cowardice and for abandoning everything to the enemy** (2.21.3), Plutarch adds the name of one of his attackers, **Cleon** (mentioned again in chap. 35 below and at *Moralia* 1065 C), and the quotation from the comic poet **Hermippus**, who had allegedly brought an indictment against Aspasia (chap. 32 above). The passage comes from his play *Fates* (fr 46 Edmonds), produced, according to Gomme, 'not . . . before the spring of 43O; but perhaps later . . .' (*Commentary on Thucycides* vol. II, p. 75). Gomme also notes that this is the first appearance in history of the notorious Cleon, who figures so largely in the pages of Thucydides and Aristophanes' *Knights* as an unworthy successor to Pericles: 'Kleon, true to the demagogue's principle enunciated by Disraeli, began his career by attacking those in power' (Gomme, *ibid.*). In the Hermippus passage, Pericles is satirized as **king of the satyrs** because these roguish followers of Dionysus typically drank to excess and preferred to make love, not war. **Teles** is otherwise unknown: 'probably some notorious coward of the day' (Holden).

Chapter 34

Plutarch gives as the reason for Pericles' absence from the first of the naval raiding expeditions on coastal areas of the Peloponnese that he had to stay behind **to watch affairs at home and keep the city under his control**. This appears to be Plutarch's own inference, and may be a correct one. On the other hand, it is questionable whether the fact that Pericles **expelled . . . the whole population of Aegina and divided up the island among the Athenians by lot** really signalled a return to the old 'demagogic' techniques of chaps. 9 to 12. The other sources provide no hint of **various subsidies and . . . grants of conquered territories** beyond the Aegina cleruchy, which is also mentioned by Thucydides (2.27.1), who explains the action by saying that the Athenians were angry with the Aeginetans because they considered them 'mainly responsible for the war' (Plutarch makes a brief mention in chap. 29 above of the Aeginetans' pressuring the Spartans to declare war). Since Aegina lay so close to the coast of the Peloponnese the Athenians, according to Thucydides, considered it 'safer' to occupy the island themselves.

That **Pericles himself led an expedition into the Megarid** in the autumn of 431 B.C., in accordance with the decree of Charinus mentioned in chap. 30 above, is also noted by Thucydides (2.31.1). Plutarch spells out more clearly than Thucydides does that Pericles' strategy of countering the Peloponnesians' invasion by seaborne raids might have succeeded **had not an act of heaven intervened**, namely, the **plague**. Plutarch draws a similar contrast between an **act of heaven** and **human calculations** in his account of the aftermath of the battle of Cannae in 216 B.C., when Hannibal inexplicably failed to follow up the victory and attack Rome, and Fabius marshalled resistance among the Romans (*Fabius* 17). It is quite likely that Pericles was held to account, as Plutarch says, for it was his policy of withdrawing from the Attic countryside and not facing the enemy in battle that led to the **herding together of the country folk into the city**, where they **lived huddled in shacks and stifling tents** ('There were no houses for those who came in, but they had to spend the summer in stifling huts,' Thucydides 2.52.2). Of course, he was not responsible for the outbreak of the epidemic, whose exact nature has defied all modern attempts at identification, in spite of the very full clinical account Thucydides gives of the course of the disease; it has been identified as everything from bubonic plague, typhoid, cholera to a particularly virulent strain of measles or toxic shock syndrome.

74

Thucydides (2.56) puts figures to this armament personally led by Pericles in the summer of 430 B.C.: fifty of the ships were supplied by Chios and Lesbos, and there were 4,000 **hoplites** and 300 **horsemen**.

The story of the **eclipse** is unhistorical, at least in the form in which Plutarch tells it. Thucydides (2.28) dates it in the preceding year, when Pericles was not personally in command; it occurred 'August 3 [431 B.C.] at about 5.22 p.m. at Athens' (Gomme, *Commentary* vol. II, p. 89; Gomme also remarks that Thucydides tells the story in a way that shows he is relying on some scientific theory of eclipses, perhaps Anaxagoras' [p. 88]). Anaxagoras is reported to have held that 'eclipses . . . of the sun [are due] to screening by the moon when it is new' (frg. 502 in Kirk, Raven & Schofield, *The Presocratic Philosophers* [2nd ed., Cambridge, 1983] p. 381). Pericles' use of scientific theory to debunk superstitious fears is also exemplified in chap. 6 above, where Anaxagoras is explicitly mentioned. Plutarch gives as the source of the story **the schools of philosophy**, which he mentions several times elsewhere in his works; that is, it would have formed part of the stock of anecdotes about philosophers of the past told by present-day lecturers, such as Plutarch's teacher Ammonius. (The anecdote occurs also in Cicero and Valerius Maximus; see Intro., sec. 3.) As a contrast we may note Nicias' superstitious reaction to the lunar eclipse of 27 Aug. 413 B.C. (Thucydides 7.50; Plutarch, *Nicias* 23).

The relative lack of success of the expedition round the coast of the Peloponnese is implied also by Thucydides, who, although he notes that the attack on Epidaurus (called **sacred** because it was a centre of the healing god Asclepius) was abortive, does not say anything about a siege (2.56.4). Thucydides tells, too, (2.59 and 65) how the Athenians took out their bitterness and angry frustration against Pericles by proceeding **to strip him of his command and punish him with a fine**. According to Diodorus (that is, presumably, Ephorus), the charge was 'something trifling' (12.45.4), although his testimony as a whole is suspect, since he gives the absurdly high figure of 80 talents as the fine. If Plato could be trusted on this kind of historical point, the charge was one of embezzlement (*Gorgias* 516 A 1-2; Plato also says 'they came close to executing him'), although Gomme seems right to question it on grounds that it 'looks like an echo of the charge against Pheidias' mentioned in chap. 32 above (*Commentary* vol. II, p. 182).

Plutarch does not say which of his sources reported the fine as **fifteen talents**. As mentioned above, Diodorus reported eighty (unless, as some scholars have suggested, the manuscripts are faulty). The **highest** known to Plutarch was **fifty** (a traditional figure, the amount imposed on Cimon's father Miltiades), and is found also in one of the spurious works among Demosthenes' speeches (*Oration* 26.6).

The tradition presented various names of Pericles' **public prosecutor**. *Idomeneus* (FGH 338 F 9; cf. chap. 1O above and Intro., sec. 3) named **Cleon**, a not implausible guess, given Hermippus' verses quoted in chap. 33 above. Aristotle's successor, **Theophrastus** and his contemporary **Heracleides of Pontus** offered two different names, relative nobodies (see Intro., sec. 3). On the whole, one sympathizes with Gomme's comment, 'it does not look as though later writers had any authority for their statements other than Thucydides and comedy' (*Commentary* vol. II, p. 182).

Chapter 36

In the famous lines by the comic writer Eupolis about Pericles' oratorical skills, Pericles 'left his sting behind in those who heard him' (frg. 98 Edmonds, v. 7; see Intro., sec. 3). The fall from popular favour he now suffered is here described in the reverse image: **the people . . . left behind their fury in their sting** (perhaps an unconscious memory of Plato's use of this same comparison, *Phaedo* 91 C 5, as Holden notes).

The story that **Xanthippus resented his father's passion for economy and the meagre allowance he was given** is very much of a piece with the gossip retailed in chap. 16. The source may be Stesimbrotus, who is cited later in this chapter. The girl whom Plutarch here identifies as Pericles' daughter-in-law, the **daughter of Tisander, Epilycus' son**, was a member of the Philaidae, Cimon's clan (Chaps. 7, 9-10, and 29 above).

It is hard to put any credence in the report that Xanthippus **borrowed money** from one of his father's friends, and that Pericles then **brought an action against** this individual. This reads like a variant of an episode in Aristophanes' *Clouds*. The remainder of the story, too, smacks of an anti-intellectual source, which emphasized the trivial nature of topics discussed (apparently endlessly) by the philosophers and litterati in Pericles' circle, men like the 'sophist' *Protagoras*. (It is perhaps no accident that Pericles' sons Xanthippus and Paralus are found among the company of Protagoras' eager listeners at Plato, *Protagoras* 315 A). The disquisition about the responsibility involved when someone is **accidentally hit . . . with a javelin and killed** in fact forms the subject of the 'Second Tetralogy' composed by the Athenian orator Antiphon, who was active in the last half of the fifth century B.C. To judge from what is known about Protagoras' writings, this kind of topic does not seem to have been among his main preoccupations, although he is credited by Plato with an interest in precision of meaning, and Plutarch may be glancing at this with the phrase 'in the strictest sense'. There are two other possible links between Protagoras and Pericles. He is reported to have remarked on Pericles' 'courage and greatness of soul' (the virtue for which Plutarch says he had Anaxagoras to thank) in not withdrawing from public life after his sons' deaths, but continuing to wear the olive-crown and white tunic instead of mourning-attire, and urging the Athenians to press on with the war (*Moralia* 118 E-F, not an authentic essay by Plutarch). And various late authorities say that, like Anaxagoras, he came under public criticism for his agnostic theories about the gods, and was banished; Plutarch elsewhere links his name with Anaxagoras' in this respect (*Life of Nicias* 23).

In the latter part of the chapter Plutarch returns to the rumour mongered by Stesimbrotus (*FGH* 107 F 11) regarding Pericles and Xanthippus' daughter, which he had already recounted in chap. 13 above. Nothing further is known about the **sister** who is mentioned among Pericles' **relatives** who fell victim to the plague along with Pericles himself. According to the testimony of Protagoras, mentioned above, Pericles' second son **Paralus** died within seven days of his elder brother, **Xanthippus**. That Pericles steadfastly refused to be crushed by the great misfortune of losing his two legitimate sons, and thus showed **greatness of spirit** which we have already been told was Anaxagoras' legacy, is the expected version and that found, as already noted, in Protagoras, in the *Miscellanies* of Valerius Maximus (see Intro., sec. 2) and in the anecdotal compilation of Aelian c. 200 A.D. It is not clear whether Plutarch had a source for his statement that Pericles' composure only finally broke **as he laid a wreath on the dead body** of Paralus, or whether this is simply a bit of dramatic heightening that Plutarch ventures to add on his own account.

Chapter 37

Thucydides reports (2.65.4) that Pericles was 'condemned to pay a fine' (which, as Gomme rightly insists, entails removal from office) but that 'not much later' he was re-elected to the generalship—that is, for 429 B.C.—the event to which Plutarch is here referring (**summoned him back** etc.). But the chronology implied by Thucydides' account does not allow for the interval of time presupposed by Plutarch's assertion that **the people tried other generals and politicians** before reinstating Pericles. Nor does the remark that **because of his grief he was lying at home in dejected spirits** square with the resoluteness we saw him displaying in the preceding chapter. Probably Plutarch is drawing on an anecdotal source here as in *Life of Alcibiades* chaps. 3 and 7 (the latter Alcibiades' famous quip that Pericles, instead of worrying about how to render public account for his actions, should be looking for ways *not* to render an account; in Diodorus [12.38] and elsewhere this is a lead-in to the Pheidias episode and the war). Pericles and his brother Ariphron had been named guardians of Alcibiades, their first cousin once removed (not nephew as Diodorus would have it), after his father Cleinias had been killed at the battle of Coroneia, along with Tolmides (see chap. 18 above).

Pericles' **law concerning children born out of wedlock** had been passed, as we learn from the Aristotelian *Constitution of Athens* (26.4), in 451 B.C. It stipulated that henceforth 'a person should not have the rights of citizenship unless both of his parents had been citizens' (*ibid.*, trans. by von Fritz and Kapp). Pericles' purpose in sponsoring this law has been much discussed. Plutarch juxtaposes it to the **40,000 measures of grain** sent to the Athenians as a **gift** by the **king of Egypt**, Psammetichus, but that is dated to 445/4 on the reliable authority of Philochorus (*FHG* 328 F 130 [Fornara 86]). It seems possible but unlikely that Pericles anticipated this dole by six years and was trying to reduce the number of potential beneficiaries. P.J. Rhodes thinks the measure reflects the premium put by Pericles on 'the Athenian-ness of the Athenian people' and that it was intended particularly to put a stop to intermarriage between Athenian men and the daughters of metics (*A Commentary on the Aristotelian 'Athenaion Politeia'* [Oxford, 1981] p. 334). The figures quoted from Philochorus are somewhat different from Plutarch's: 30,000 **measures of grain**, 4,760 **people were convicted** and 14,240 **retained their citizenship**.

Plutarch's reference to Pericles' **pride and presumption**, now humbled, takes us back to the young politician, unsure of himself and therefore arrogant, of the earlier part of the *Life*.

The fact of citizenship was authenticated when a new father took his infant son or daughter to a gathering of members of his **phratry** (a sort of religious club) who attested to the legitimacy of the infant and added his or her name to the phratry-list. Plutarch concludes the chapter by remarking on the unhappy end to which the young Pericles came when in 406 B.C. he was **put to death by popular decree along with his fellow generals** after the Athenian defeat at **Arginusae**—the proceedings at which Socrates refused to preside because of the illegality of trying defendants *en masse* rather than individually (Plato, *Apology* 32 B). Before holding the generalship in this fatal year, the younger Pericles had been *Hellenotamias*, one of the treasurers of the Delian Confederacy, in 410 B.C.; for Eupolis' reference to his dubious citizen-status in *Demes* see note to chap. 24 above.

Chapter 38

Pericles' death is to be placed in the autumn of 429 B.C. It is not clear whether Plutarch is drawing on some particular source for the description of his illness as **not a violent or acute attack** but a gradual wasting away, or whether this is merely an assumption based on the story which follows. He adds the interesting detail from **Theophrastus'** *Ethics* (fr. L21 Fortenbaugh), with its pathetic anecdote of the **charm . . . hung round his neck** (Holden notes that at *Moralia* 920 B 'charms' are mentioned along with purifications and dreams as among the expedients to which those suffering from chronic disease typically but ineffectually seek recourse). Theophrastus had been cited in chaps. 23 and 35 above for specific details in Pericles' career.

The source cannot be traced for Plutarch's statement that Pericles **had won no less than nine victories as Athens' commander-in-chief** (repeated at Comparison 2 [= *Fabius* 29]).

The anecdote with which the chapter ends was part of the standard repertoire (*Moralia* 543 C and in the spurious 'Sayings of Kings and Commanders' 186 D). Its import is not exactly clear, for men certainly had died in expeditions led by Pericles, in spite of Plutarch's attempts to turn all his military exploits into unqualified successes. Perhaps he meant that none of his undertakings had been total disasters, such as the survivors might justly have reproached Pericles for having undertaken.

Chapter 39

Plutarch closes the *Life* with an extended eulogy of what he sees as Pericles' particular virtues: a sense of justice (the word could also be translated 'reasonableness' 'basic decency'), serene temper and an Anaxagorean **greatness of spirit**. He had in chap. 8 above given various possible grounds (not all of them flattering) for the **pretentious and childish nickname . . . 'Olympian'**; he now puts forward the most exalted interpretation possible, **gracious** [the same word as was translated by 'justice' above] . . . **pure and uncorrupt**, like the fabled Mt. Olympus, dwelling place of the immortal gods. Plutarch digresses momentarily to comment on the discrepancy between standard descriptions of Olympus as **a calm, untroubled place**—see, for example, Homer, *Odyssey* 6.43-46—and the unedifying tales of the gods' behaviour, **filled with discontent, malice, anger, and other passions**, an anomaly similar to that pointed out by Plato in Book 2 of *The Republic* for his own philosophical purposes.

The chapter concludes with a final theme borrowed from Thucydides (2.65.10; Holden cites also the Aristotelian *Constitution of Athens*, chap. 28), the sharp contrast between the high standards of Pericles and his less worthy successors. It is a view based perhaps less on fact than on class- prejudice or a philosophical model of declination or degeneration from an ideal to a corrupt mode of being, but Plutarch puts a fitting capstone on his eulogistic but also fair and balanced portrait of a leader whose style of government could be viewed, according to whether one disapproved of or admired his policies, either as a **monarchy and a tyranny** or as **the saving bulwark of the state.**

Endnotes

Endnote A   *Pericles and the Comic Poets*

We must form our views of 'Old Comedy,' that is, the earliest type of ancient Athenian comedy to survive, mainly from the works of Aristophanes, since all but a few citations and papyrus fragments of the other writers of this type of drama have perished. From Aristophanes' own works, however, it is clear that prominent public persons, often though not invariably generals and politicians, were fair game for a theatrical satire that was often vicious (Cleon in *The Knights*, for example; Socrates in *The Clouds* that the targets were not always political figures). Plutarch gives excerpts from several writers of Old Comedy who brought Pericles and his associates onto the stage in various laughable disguises, and made fun of him for his personal appearance, his overbearing and allegedly 'tyrannical' manner, his liaison with Aspasia, and the escapades of some of his close associates like Lampon and Pheidias. This note presents a brief survey of these poets and those of their plays that touched on various aspects of Pericles and his circle.

CRATINUS who, as a comic writer, ranked with Aristophanes and Eupolis, lived from about 490 B.C. to the late 420s. He is best remembered as the winner over Aristophanes' *Clouds* in 423 B.C., a defeat which Aristophanes did not take lying down (*Clouds*, second version, vv. 520ff.). Of his 28 known titles, some half-dozen seem to have dealt more or less exclusively with Pericles. The earliest reference that can be dated is the passage from an unnamed play cited by Plutarch in *Per.* 13, in which Pericles is ridiculed for (apparently) not moving quickly enough to complete the Long Walls. The point of the joke is unclear. Plutarch cites the lines in connection with the third or 'middle' long wall to Peiraeus, and reminds his readers that Plato had quoted Socrates at *Gorgias* 455 E as saying that 'he himself had listened to Pericles haranguing the Athenians about the Middle Wall'. The only date at which these pieces of information can be made to converge historically (that is, if Plato is not just making it all up or misremembering, as he sometimes does) is about 444-442 B.C., when there is inscriptional evidence for wall-building activity at Athens (Gomme, *Commentary* vol. I, p. 312 n. 3; Dodds' note on the *Gorgias* passage). Whether Pericles was in reality dragging his feet and, if so, what his reasons may have been, we have no way of knowing.

The fragments of Cratinus' *Runaway Women* (*Drapetides*) are tantalizingly full of what seem to be political references, but too little survives for a certain reconstruction. Here, the main butt of Cratinus' attack seems to have been Lampon, who was one of the official 'Thurii-priests' who led the colony to Thurii c. 443 B.C. (mentioned briefly at the end of *Per.* 11). J. M. Edmonds may be right to suggest that the significance of the play's title in the feminine gender is that the colonists were 'feminised for their supposed effeminacy or cowardice' (*The Fragments of Attic Comedy* Vol. I [Leiden: Brill, 1957] p. 38 note a; references to the comic fragments are to this collection and also, where available, to the new edition by R. Kassel and C. Austin), although it is a little difficult to see how participation in this grand venture to S. Italy could be construed as cowardice. Lampon was dubbed a 'sacrificial axe-gatherer', which does not sound like a compliment. The main character in the play was Theseus, of whom Thucydides (2.15) gives an idealized picture as the prehistoric king of Athens who 'synoecized' or unified the outlying villages of Attica into a single polis. He is addressed as 'son of Pandion, king of the rich-clodded city [sarcasm, or a pun suggesting 'excessively fond of voting'], do you know what city we mean?' Theseus replies, 'Yes, and they're playing the 'Dog-and-City' game,' by which he seems to mean 'the Athenians are playing politics, as usual' (some have seen a reference to the ostracism of Thucydides, son of Melesias; see the end of *Per.* ch. 14). Another line referred to certain unnamed individuals who 'took part in civil strife and wanted to be somebody'. A general named Xenophon, one of Pericles' colleagues in the war against Samos, also came under fire: 'From a clear sky I shall cast lightning on the buggery of Xenophon the mouse'. The speaker expresses himself in terms used by Zeus in Homer; since, as we saw, Pericles was nicknamed 'The Olympian' and was ridiculed for what was perceived as a Zeus-like arrogance, it is possible that the character who spoke the lines (Theseus?) allegorically represented Pericles.

Cratinus' *Thracian Women* dealt with the worship of the exotic Thracian goddess Bendis, whose newly-imported festival is mentioned at the beginning of Plato's *Republic*. As the excerpt quoted in chap. 13 above shows, Cratinus ridiculed Pericles as 'squill-headed Zeus', and presented the extravagant and ludicrous conception of his wearing the umbrella-roofed Odeion to cover his elongated head. The play probably dates from the late 440s, when the Odeion had recently been completed and, with the ostracism of Thucydides son of Melesias, all effective opposition to Pericles' policies was removed. Gilbert Norwood plausibly suggested that 'the tile' mentioned in line 3 of the excerpt has a double meaning, a roof tile from the newly constructed building and the clay sherd used in ostracism-voting (*Greek Comedy*, 1963 ed., pp. 134-5). Probably from somewhat later comes *Cheirons*, whose chorus was composed of multiple representations of the centaur who tutored Achilles. Cratinus seems to have regarded it as his best play, for he has the chorus comment that the author had been working on it for over two years (fr. 237 = 255) and somewhere in it a challenge was issued to his competitors to come up with a better one, if they could. The anti-Periclean tenor of the passage quoted by Plutarch in chap. 3 above is obvious: Pericles-Zeus (the identification is made certain by the modified Homeric tag, 'Head-gatherer') is the offspring of ugly parents, Stasis or Civil strife and Cronos (or Time, Chronos), and is himself a tyrant. The plot is difficult to reconstruct, but Cratinus seems to have read the Athenians a lesson on the glories of the past, the advantages of an educational system long since discarded, which could aptly be symbolized by a whole chorus of Achilles' tutors. Solon the Wise Man was conjured up from the dead with an authentic-sounding but ludicrous incantation, 'Come, now, turn Dawn-ward and take in your hands a great . . . squill,' Pericles' head again (fr. 232 = 250). This is the first play in which we can detect a satirical reference to Pericles' mistress, Aspasia, who was attacked in coarse and abusive terms (chap. 24 above). By a strange mixture of political allegories, she was also ridiculed in this play as 'Queen Omphale' (fr. 241 B = 259). Allegations of bribe-taking were laid against these 'divinities' (fr. 244 = 261), but whether Pericles and Aspasia were directly implicated is unclear, nor can we be sure what action was being alluded to. Some have seen a reference to the institution of payment for public service (see Endnote B), or the the exaction of tribute from the allies.

The identification of Pericles with Zeus again figures prominently in Cratinus' *Nemesis* (chap. 3 above). In the play, as Eratosthenes reports, 'Zeus made love to Nemesis in the shape of a swan, after alighting at Rhamnous in Attica, and from the egg was hatched Helen'. Commentators have seen here a connection with the construction of a temple to Nemesis in the rural district of Rhamnous on the northeast coast of Attica soon after 440 B.C., and the dedication of a cult statue by Agoracritus, Pheidias' pupil (Pausanias 1.33.2-3, where Pheidias is named as sculptor, to be corrected on the basis of Pliny, *Natural Histories* 36.17; for the date, R. Meiggs and D. Lewis, *A Selection of Greek Historical Inscriptions* [Oxford, 1969] 53). Cratinus seems to have combined the alternate version of Helen's birth with the more usual one of her birth from Leda. In the course of the play the egg was apparently carried to Leda in Sparta, where Zeus asked her to hatch it for him. In terms of the allegory Leda, of course, will have represented Aspasia and the egg will be Pericles' son by her, the younger Pericles.

Some scholars have suggested that Pericles' response to these attacks on himself and his circle of friends was to impose the 'law against comedy', mentioned by a Scholiast on Aristophanes'

Acharnians (v. 67) as having been in effect from 440/39 to 437/6 B.C. It has been pointed out that Cratinus' comment, already referred to, that he had been working on *Cheirons* for 'over two years' (fr. 237 Edm. = 255 K/A), may allude to the fact that the production of comedies had been forbidden during the preceding period. Too little is known about this law, however, to make such speculation useful. We do not know, for example, whether it forbade all comedy or only personal attacks of the kind Cratinus seems to have specialized in, and Pericles' sponsorship of the law, though it might appear probable, is nowhere directly attested.

In *Riches* (*Ploutoi*) Cratinus' satire was directed at the general Hagnon, Pericles' associate against Samos and founder of Amphipolis in 437. The 'golden age' of Cronos was extolled and, by contrast, the present reign of Pericles probably condemned. In an extended passage the Chorus sing, 'It is the beginning of a new tyranny and Demos (the People) rules' (fr. 162 A = 171, vv. 23-4). There is also a cryptic reference to 'Aeginetan cakes in the wrestling-rings,' which may have something to do with the fact that certain members of Cimon's aristocratic circle, like Melesias, were famed wrestling-coaches who had trained a number of Aeginetan victors in the 470s and 460s. From this period also may date *Nomoi* or *Laws*, whose chorus consisted of old and decrepit embodiments of Athens' laws, possibly led by Solon (in one fragment an unnamed speaker echoes a phrase of Solon's, when he refers to some individuals as 'each of you a fox who takes bribes'). In fr. 132 Edm. (= 139 Kassel-Austin) 'Tyrrhenian sandals' were mentioned which, according to the source, are to be identified with the sandals with which Pheidias shod his statue of Athena Parthenos. If this is correct, the play would date from some year after 438/7 when, on the most plausible chronology, Pheidias completed his statue. In that case, it is possible that Cratinus was making a charge against Pheidias similar to those recorded by Plutarch in chap. 31.

The plot of Cratinus' *Dionysalexandros*, about which we are relatively well informed, was ingenious. Dionysus—and we are reminded of Aristophanes' *Frogs*—comically fills in for Paris at the Judgement of the Goddesses. After awarding the prize to Aphrodite he sails to Sparta and brings Helen back to Troy, but when he learns that the Greeks are in pursuit, he hides Helen in a basket and disguises himself as a ram. Paris arrives, detects them both and orders them to be taken and handed over to the Greeks. Helen objects and Paris decides to make her his wife but hand over Dionysus. The god's constant attendants, the satyrs, escort him away with assurances that they will never desert him. Our source of information about all this is a papyrus fragment from Oxyrhynchus (663), which adds the revealing comment, 'in the play Pericles is satirized most convincingly by innuendo for having involved Athens in the war' (probably the

Peloponnesian War, although the Samian War cannot be ruled out). Dionysus-Alexander's rape of Helen will then stand for Pericles' 'rape' of Aspasia, and the Trojan War for the Peloponnesian (or Samian), a comic concept which was later to be picked up by Aristophanes in *Acharnians* (chap. 30 above).

Upon re-examination of the above papyrus and an additional papyrus fragment (*P. Oxy.* 2806, published in 1971), E.W. Handley made the attractive suggestion that the play dealt in a satirical way with the theme of 'generating an instant family'. This may touch on the problem Pericles was having in securing from the Assembly a reversal of his own citizenship law so that his illegitimate son by Aspasia could become his legal heir. The allusion, however, is not quite secure, for it is uncertain when exactly *Dionysalexandros* was produced. Some scholars place it in the spring of 430 B.C., that is, before the outbreak of the plague in the following summer which deprived Pericles of legitimate heirs, while others feel that it is more probably to be dated to 429 B.C., when a satirical reference to the younger Pericles would have been very timely.

In contrast to Cratinus, of whose work the fragments allow us to form a fairly good idea, other comedians who attacked Pericles are hardly more than names. TELECLEIDES, to whom are ascribed 8 or 9 titles, made fun of the shape of Pericles' head (chap. 3) and, more significantly, ridiculed the thoroughgoing nature of his control of Athens' foreign policy and her dealings with her allies (chap. 16). In the *Hesiods* of perhaps 430 B.C. he mentioned a Corinthian lady named Chrysilla who was 'the lover of Pericles the Olympian' (fr. 17 Edmonds), and in the *Amphictyons* (fr. 6 Edm.) reference was made to the Diopeithes who, according to Plutarch (chap. 32), tried to assail Pericles indirectly, with a charge of atheism against Anaxagoras. HERMIPPUS, said to have produced 40 plays of which 10 titles are known, was clearly casting a jibe at Pericles with his remark about 'a head as big as a pumpkin' (fr. 79 Edmonds) and 'Say there, tickle my head, will you?' (fr. 78). Since, according to the well-known myth (portrayed, among other places, on the east pediment of the Parthenon), Athena was gestated in Zeus' swollen head from which she finally sprang, fully armed, into life with the help of a blow from Hephaestus' axe, Edmonds ascribes these fragments to the play entitled *Birth of Athena*. He sees a connection with Pheidias' statue of Athena Promachos, dedicated c. 440, or the Parthenos of 438, and suggests a Zeus-Pericles identification. From *Moirai* or *Fates* Plutarch in chap. 33 quotes the long passage making fun of Pericles as 'king of the satyrs' and referring to attacks on him by Cleon. Plutarch also (chap. 32) reports that Hermippus brought a suit against Aspasia, but the nature of the charge, *procuring free-born Athenian women for Pericles and receiving them into her house*, has suggested to some scholars that Plutarch or his source had misunderstood what was in

actual fact a passage in one of Hermippus' plays. Allusions—
admittedly rather veiled—have been discovered in the works of
PHERECRATES (17 or 18 plays; victories recorded at the City
Dionysia and Lenaia) to 'strangulation' of the allies (fr. 21 Edm.) and
perhaps the alleged bribe of ten talents paid by Pericles to the
Spartans (fr. 151; cf. chap. 23 above). From one of his plays entitled
Old Women comes a tantalizing line, 'with the Athenian women
themselves and their feminine allies' (fr. 34).

Besides those comedians whom Plutarch names, he also refers in
several places to 'comic writers' for various satirical comments:
Aspasia was the 'new Omphale' and 'Deianeira' to Pericles' Heracles
(chap. 24); Pheidias used his art-works or Pyrilampes his peacocks to
lure women for Pericles' sexual enjoyment (chap. 13). Interestingly,
this latter joke may have been picked up by Aristophanes who in a
lost play referred to someone, probably Pericles, 'rearing a kite [the
Greek word is *iktinos*, the same as the architect named in chap. 13]
with an all-seeing eye for his snatchings' (fr. 628 Edm.). These
attacks, however painful they may have been, would not have
rankled Pericles as much as the comic writers' labeling of his friends
as the 'new Peisistratids' and 'their call upon him to take the oath that
he will never set himself up as a tyrant' (chap. 16). Here was a thrust
with a real point to it, and one which must have cut the more deeply
because it contained an element of truth.

With Pericles' death in the autumn of 429, his attractiveness as a
butt of satire was much diminished. Cratinus was forced to turn on
Cleon in his *Seriphians*. EUPOLIS, the third of the great comic triad,
brought out his first comedy in 429, when he was only 17; 19 titles of
his works are known, with 7 of which he won first prize. Wilamowitz
detected a reference to Pyrilampes' peacocks in a citation from his
work *Men exempt from Service* (fr. 36, with Edmonds' note). His
Prospaltians drew its title from a deme that was part of Acamantis,
Pericles' tribe, which was also mentioned in the play (fr. 244 A, line
21), and in some unknown context Aspasia was referred to as 'Helen'
(fr. 249). Quite extensive papyrus fragments survive from *Demes* (c.
412 B.C.), from which Plutarch in chap. 3 cites a line which shows
that Pericles was among the great men of Athens' past summoned up
from Hades along with Solon, Miltiades and Aristeides. A long
fragment (117) makes the contrast explicit: 'Our generals used to
come from the finest, richest families, prayed to like gods . . . Now
we choose offscourings to be our generals'. There was a question by
Pericles about his 'bastard son' with the response, referring to his
mother, Aspasia, as 'the whore' (chap. 24 above). It was in this play
that there occurred the famous praise of Pericles' ability to 'cast a
spell' on his audience (fr. 98; cf. Intro., sec. 3). It is unknown how the
appearance of Peisistratus as 'King' (fr. 96) was worked into the plot,
or what relevance this might have had to Pericles' position.

The working life of the comic poet PLATO fell between 427 and 385 B.C. His reputation as an outstanding writer of 'middle' comedy (the style between Aristophanes' early works and Menander) seems fully justified. Thirty titles are recorded, and many of the fragments show him intensely concerned with the politics of the last quarter of the fifth century (thus, *Islands*—probably the island-members of the Empire—*Metics*, *Hyperbolus*, *Cleophon*, *Peisander*). The couplet cited by Plutarch in chap. 4 (fr. 191 Edmonds) from an unnamed play cast Damon as Pericles' 'Cheiron'; Plato perhaps borrowed his idea from Cratinus' *Cheirons*, discussed above.

ARISTOPHANES' play, *Babylonians*, produced in 426 B.C., from which Plutarch cites a line at the end of chap. 26, may have been critical of Pericles' treatment of the Samian captives. Otherwise, apart from two extended passages to be discussed below, there are just passing allusions in the extant plays, such as the exchange between father and son in *Clouds*. Son: 'What have you done with your shoes, you foolish man?' Father: 'Just like Pericles, I used them "for necessary expenses" ' (*Clouds* 858-9; cf. chap. 23 above). A 'sheep-seller' is mentioned in *Knights* (v. 132), and this has generally been seen as a reference to Lysicles, whom Aspasia married after Pericles' death, although I have questioned this identification in my note on chap. 24 above. The well-known story about Agariste's dream just before Pericles' birth (Herodotus 6.131; see chap. 3 above) is alluded to satirically in *Knights* (424 B.C.) when the Paphlagonian slave, who allegorically represents Cleon, quotes from an oracle, 'She is a woman, but will bear a lion in sacred Athens who will—fight for the demos against many mosquitoes' (vv. 1037-8). The ostracism of Thucydides son of Melesias crops up in *Wasps* (vv. 947 ff.) and Lampon and his soothsayer's goose get a mention in *Birds* (v. 521).

Two passages form exceptions to this general silence on Aristophanes' part, and both have to do with Pericles' alleged responsibility for the Peloponnesian War. The first, *Acharnians* 524ff., makes Pericles react in Olympian fashion to some unnamed—and probably fictional—Megarians' snatching of two prostitutes from Aspasia's brothel; Pericles is then said to have passed the Megarian Decree in reprisal (see chap. 30 above, with notes, and Endnote D, 'The Megarian Decrees'). The second passage occurs in *Peace* of 421 B.C. It charges that when his friend Pheidias got into trouble (Aristophanes does not specify the reason, but something like the charges recounted in chap. 31 must be meant), Pericles 'threw in a small spark, the Megarian Decree, and blew up such a fiery war that all the Greeks wept from the smoke' (vv. 609-11). Our suspicions should be aroused by the echoes of this passage in Plutarch's ostensibly historical account in chap. 32: '. . . now that the war was threatening and smouldering, we are told that he deliberately fanned it into

flame. He hoped in this way to dispel the charges against him . . .'
What started life as a joke in Aristophanes has found its way into
Plutarch (perhaps *via* Ephorus) as sober fact. There is an added
difficulty in that Aristophanes' joke, to be comically plausible,
supposes no very long stretch of time between Pheidias' troubles and
Pericles' alleged intervention with the Megarian Decree. Now the
Scholiast on this passage of Aristophanes dates Pheidias' trial to
(apparently; see Endnote E) 438 B.C., on the authority of Philochorus. Can we therefore infer that the Megarian Decree, or the first
Decree if there was a succession of them, was passed around 438? On
the currently accepted view, Pericles did not take action against the
Megarians until considerably later (see Endnote D). The chronological implications of *Peace* 609ff. can always be evaded by insisting
that comic writers need not be very careful about chronology, or that
Aristophanes has 'foreshortened' the period of time between the
events to which he is making theatrical fun. Still, I confess to a certain
uneasiness in dismissing this particular piece of evidence so high-
handedly. Events for which a ludicrous cause-and-effect relationship
is postulated ought at least to have a possible nexus in time, or the
joke collapses, and Aristophanes must have known that.

Bibliography

The only recent treatment is in German, Joachim Schwarze, *Die Beurteilung
des Perikles durch die attische Komödie und ihre historische und historio-
graphische Bedeutung* [*Zetemata* No. 51] (Munich, C. H. Beck, 1971) ; cf. my
review in *Athenaeum* 51 (1973) 429-434. In general on the comic poets:
Katherine Lever, *The Art of Greek Comedy* (London, Methuen, 1956);
Gilbert Norwood, *Greek Comedy* (originally published 1931; paperbound
ed. N.Y., Hill & Wang, 1963).

Endnote B   *Did Pericles 'transform the whole people into wage-earners' (chap. 12)? The building program and the benefits of empire.*

Plutarch's picture of Pericles as a dispenser of largesse in the manner of Peisistratus is taken over from some earlier writer, most probably Theopompus. This view of Pericles as one who kept a tight hold on the purse-strings of the Empire so he could dispense its benefits (and so win votes away from his rivals, like Cimon and Thucydides son of Melesias) probably contains a measure of truth. The question is, how much? The best way of approaching this topic is to look at specific measures attributed to Pericles, then at the archaeological evidence for Athens' building program during his years in office. Thus we can arrive at some very general idea of his benefactions to the people.

In chap. 9 Plutarch refers to the story told in the *Constitution of Athens* ascribed to Aristotle (27.4) that to counteract the largesse of Cimon, Pericles turned to the musician and philosopher Damonides (who may be the same as 'Damon' of chap. 4), who advised him to 'give the masses what was their own.' What this meant in practice, Plutarch explains, was 'allowances for public festivals, fees for jury service, and other grants and gratuities' by which he 'succeeded in bribing the masses wholesale'. Of the two forms of payment specifically mentioned, only that paid to members of juries (originally 2 obols daily, raised to 3 by Cleon) is, in the opinion of most scholars, certainly Periclean. P.J. Rhodes remarks of the so-called 'theoric' allowance, a grant 'to citizens at the time of the major festivals [the Dionysia and Panathenaia are elsewhere mentioned specifically], to cover the costs of their theatre tickets,' that 'there is no contemporary evidence to support a fifth-century date' (*A Commentary on the Aristotelian 'Athenaion Politeia'* [Oxford, 1981] 514). The introduction of pay for other kinds of public service might be attributable to Pericles. With regard to payment for attendance at Assembly meetings, however, there is sufficient evidence to show that this was not introduced until the closing years of the fifth century, by a certain Aghyrrios; the amount was one obol at first, raised to 3 obols by 393 B.C., and of course paid only on days when the Assembly met, and probably only to a limited number, the first 'so-many'—Rhodes suggests 6,000—to enter. The bouleutic fee of 5 obols on the other hand, which Rhodes thinks 'is likely to have been instituted before rather than after the outbreak of the Peloponnesian War' (*Commentary on the Aristotelian Ath. Pol.*, p. 304), might conceivably have been due to Pericles' initiatives. (For a *terminus post quem* Rhodes elsewhere suggests 'hardly . . . before the 450s,' *The Athenian Boule* [Oxford, 1972] 5.) The jurist Ulpian, writing in the early third century A.D., attributes to Pericles, besides the 'theoric' payment already discussed, the introduction of payment for military service; what evidence he had (if any) is unknown. The figure for the Athenian army at the outbreak of the war with Sparta was 29,000 combined combat and garrison troops (Thucydides 2.13.6). Their rate of pay is a matter of dispute among scholars. Thucydides reports (3.17.4) that the Athenian hoplites at Potidaea in 428 were paid two drachmas a day, one for the man himself and one for his attendant. This has been taken as the regular rate by A.H.M. Jones (*Athenian Democracy* [Oxford, 1964] p. 7 with n. 27, p. 32 n. 54), while others, like Gomme, believe that this rate of pay was exceptional, and that the normal rate for hoplites, as (apparently) for oarsmen in the fleet and unskilled construction workers, was 3 obols (a half-drachma) a day.

In chap. 11 Plutarch asserts that Pericles 'sent out 60 triremes to cruise every year, in which many of the citizens served with pay for eight months'. First, it should be noted that rowers in Athens' crews did not have to be Athenian citizens; the opportunity for service in the imperial fleet was clearly one of the attractions for ordinary men in the allied cities (the Corinthian speaker at the Peloponnesian Congress in 432 B.C. proposes using money borrowed from the treasuries at the shrines of Olympia and Delphi to 'induce defection of the Athenians' foreign sailors with higher pay', Thuc.1.121.2). Furthermore, serious doubt has been cast on this figure of 60 ships in service for 8 months of the year (see n. on chap 11 above, and S.K. Eddy, 'Athens Peacetime Navy. . .,' *GRBS* 9 [1968] 141-56). Andrewes remarks that, even at the reduced rate of 'the two obols of pre-war jurors, . . . that makes . . . 160 T per year,' a figure which he calls 'absurd' ('The Opposition to Perikles,' *Journal of Hellenic Studies* 98 [1978] 3). Whichever figure is chosen, the total annual expenditure still seems enormous, especially in view of the fact that additional money would have been required to pay the crews of the remaining ships in Athens' fleet, which totalled 300, if and as the need arose to put them into active service.

In discussing Pericles' building program, Plutarch has an unnamed opponent voice the objection that Athens was like some vain woman decking herself out with. . . . temples worth millions in money (chap. 12; a more literal rendering of the Greek is 'thousand-talent temples'). Before we proceed to even a rough estimate of the costs involved, it will be necessary to get some idea of the scope of Pericles' grand design, for it cannot seriously be doubted that he was behind, or at least tacitly approved of, even those construction projects with which his name is not directly connected in the sources (a detailed account of these buildings can be found in Boersma, *Athenian Building Policy from 561/0 to 405/4 B.C.* [Groningen, 1970] pp. 66ff.). A list of the architectural projects that can be called 'Periclean' in this extended sense would include: the Parthenon, Propylaia and Odeion, as mentioned by Plutarch; the Hephaestion (known popularly today, but inaccurately, as the 'Theseion') overlooking the

Athenian Agora; a *telesterion*, or structure where initiates viewed the Mysteries, at Eleusis; a temple to Poseidon at Sunium; a temple to Ares and Athena at Acharnae; a sanctuary to Nemesis at Rhamnous (see 'Endnote A' above, for a possible connection with Cratinus' comedy, *Nemesis*); a temple to Demeter at Thorikos. In addition, Pericles is said to have built a 'stoa for the sale of flour' in Peiraeus, which is mentioned only in a literary source, a Scholiast on Aristophanes' *Acharnians* 548, and members of his family were in some way connected with the building referred to in the document known as the 'Springhouse Decree' (see note on chap. 14 above). Some scholars would also assign to the Periclean period the rebuilding of the Theatre of Dionysus and its conversion from a somewhat makeshift wooden building to a permanent, and much more elaborate, stone structure, but the date of this is in dispute and it perhaps did not occur until some time in the last two decades of the century. In the case of only one of these structures, the Propylaia, do the ancient sources preserve a definite cost. Heliodorus of Athens, who wrote a work 'On the Acropolis', or 'On Dedications on the Acropolis', probably some time in the second century B.C., is quoted for the statement that the Propylaia took 6 years to build (that is, 437 to 432 inclusive) and cost 2,012 talents. This has been questioned, by Gomme and others, on grounds that the much larger and more elaborate Parthenon would have had to cost proportionately more — perhaps three times as much — and yet the implication of the financial accounting given by Pericles on the eve of the war is that 3,700 talents had been spent 'to pay for the Propylaia and other public buildings, and for Potidaea' (Thuc. 2.13.3). Now at 2.70.2 Thucydides gives 2,000+ talents as the cost of the siege of Potidaea, of which Gomme reckons perhaps 800-1,000 talents will have been spent by the time of Pericles' remarks in 431 B.C. 'This would leave [Gomme remarks] rather less than 3,000 tal. for the sum spent on the Propylaia and other buildings' (*Commentary* vol. II, p. 22). It therefore seems impossible that some two thousand of these could have been expended on the Propylaia alone. Similarly, R.W. Stanier ('The Cost of the Parthenon', Journal of Hellenic Studies 73 [1953] 68-76) compared the figures preserved in the inscribed building accounts for the temple of Asklepios at Epidaurus, built in 380-375 B.C., and the more fragmentary Erechtheum accounts. On a proportional calculation of stonework, ceilings, roofs and grates, and sculptured decoration, between the Asklepieion and the Parthenon, Stanier came up with a figure of 469 talents for the Parthenon or, with allowance for a different conversion-scale of money between 440 and 380 B.C., 640 talents at most, with the Propylaia costing perhaps 200 talents. Even if these figures are not precisely accurate, it is still likely, as Gomme wrote, 'that the cost of the Propylaia and the Parthenon must be reckoned in hundreds, not thousands of talents'

(*Commentary* vol. II, p. 22). An attempt was made by the authors of the *Athenian Tribute Lists* to keep Heliodorus' apparently precise figure of 2,012 talents, but reinterpret it as covering the costs of all the Periclean building on the Acropolis, which would leave something less than 1,000 talents for the buildings outside Athens itself, like the Ares temple, and the constructions at Rhamnous, Eleusis and Sunium.

It is difficult enough to arrive at a reasonable estimate of the total costs involved, but far more so to suggest any kind of figure, however conjectural, for the number of people employed in, and so benefiting from, these projects. In a memorable chapter Plutarch catalogues the variety of occupations involved: '. . . carpenter, modeller, copper-smith, stone-mason, dyer, worker in gold and ivory, painter, embroiderer, and engraver, and besides these the carriers and suppliers of the materials, such as merchants, sailors, and pilots for the sea-borne traffic, and waggon-makers, trainers of draught animals, and drivers of everything that came by land. There were also rope-makers, weavers, leatherworkers, roadbuilders and miners.' (*Pericles* chap. 12). Unfortunately, no exact figures survive, although it must be pointed out, once again, that, if they did, they, too, would include (like the sailors) non-citizens, resident aliens and even slaves since, as the Erechtheum records show, no attempt was made to exclude them in the offer of employment. On the basis of the surviving accounts and practical considerations, A. Burford concluded for the Parthenon alone that, although there were perhaps 'only 200 men on the site at any one time . . ., something over 1,000 men were concerned in the project altogether', and that over a period of 15 years ('The Builders of the Parthenon', *Greece & Rome* Suppl. to vol. X [1963] p. 34). Of course this figure would have to be multiplied many times to take account of all the other buildings constructed under Pericles. Gomme based his caluculations on a total of 2,200 talents spent on building projects in Attica over a period of 16 years (447/6 to 432/1 B.C.), to give 825,000 drachmae yearly, divided by 250 working days, to equal 3,300 drachmae in daily pay for workers. At a wage-rate of 1 dr. per man per day (the figure for skilled workers in the Erechtheum accounts), 'an average of about 3,300 men were employed' (*Commentary* vol. II, p. 46). Gomme felt, however, that some individuals like skilled sculptors and those who transported materials over sea probably were paid more, and so the daily rate might average out to 1½ dr. Thus, he concluded that 'the average daily number employed would be 2,200: a sufficiently impressive figure' (*ibid.*, 47).

Xenophon mentions the sum of 'not less than 1,000 talents of annual income to the city from internal and foreign sources' (*Anabasis* 7.1.27), which scholars usually distinguish as 600 from abroad (the actual tribute collected, which was, according to the inscribed

Tribute-Quota lists, less than 400 talents, plus other income from imperial sources, such as war-indemnity, as at Samos, and income from confiscated land) and 400 from domestic sources. The *Constitution of Athens* ascribed to Aristotle attempts a breakdown of the beneficiares of this income: '. . . out of the income derived from the contributions made by the allies and from internal levies more than 20,000 persons were maintained. For there were 6,000 judges, 1,600 bowmen, 1,200 cavalry men, 500 Councilmen, 500 guards of the Dockyards plus 50 guards on the Acropolis, about 700 state officials at home and about 700 abroad' (*Ath. Pol.* 24.3, trans. von Fritz and Kapp). 'It must be remembered,' Rhodes points out in his note on this passage, 'that many of the men listed, such as jurors and bouleutae [councilmen], were paid only for the days when then actually served' (*A Commentary on the Aristotelian 'Athenaion Politeia'* [Oxford, 1981] 302). Rhodes also feels that the figure '700 abroad' is simply miscopied from the previous phrase, and should be emended. Others, however, such as M.I. Finley ('The Fifth-century Athenian Empire', p. 109), accept it, and even Rhodes admits that 'we cannot begin to estimate how many Athenian officials with postings abroad there may have been at any time during the existence of the Delian League' (*Commentary*, p. 305).

We are left, then, with a picture, not always verifiable in specific detail but clear enough in its general outline, of an Athens incalculably richer than she would have been without her Empire, and of numbers of individuals (not necessarily restricted to Athenian citizens) to be reckoned in the thousands, who made their living off this income. Plutarch's view that Pericles transformed the whole people into wage-earners is essentially correct.

Bibliography

J.S. Boersma, *Athenian Building Policy from 561/0 to 405/4 B.C.* ·(Groningen, 1970)

A. Burford, 'The Builders of the Parthenon,' in *Parthenos and Parthenon* [= *Greece and Rome*, Supp. to vol. X] (Oxford, 1963) pp. 23-35

A.W. Gomme, *A Historical Commentary on Thucydides* vol. II (Oxford, 1956) pp. 20-26

R.W. Stanier, 'The Cost of the Parthenon', *Journal of Hellenic Studies* 73 (1953) 68-76

M.I. Finley, 'The Fifth-century Athenian Empire: a balance sheet', in P. Garnsey and C. Whittaker, edd., *Imperialism in the Ancient World* (Cambridge, 1978) 103-126 (= *Economy and Society in Ancient Greece* [London, 1981] 41-61)

A.H.M. Jones, 'The Economic Basis of the Athenian Democracy', in Jones, *Athenian Democracy* (Oxford, 1964) pp. 3-20

S.K. Eddy, 'Athens' Peacetime Navy in the Age of Perikles', *Greek, Roman & Byzantine Studies* 9 (1968) 141-156

D. Blackman, 'The Athenian Navy and Allied Naval Contributions in the Pentecontaetia', *GRBS* 10 (1969) 179-216

M.H. Hansen, 'Seven Hundred Archai in Classical Athens', *GRBS* 21 (1980) 151-173

Ron. K. Unz, 'The Surplus of the Athenian Phoros', *GRBS* 26 (1985) 21-42

Endnote C *Some Disputed Documents*

Plutarch (*Per.* 17) is our only source for the Panhellenic Congress which Pericles proposed to summon to discuss 'the Greek sanctuaries which had been burned by the Persians; the sacrifices owed to the gods on behalf of Hellas to fulfil the vows made when they were fighting the Persians; and the security of the seas, so that all ships could sail them without fear and keep the peace.' The genuineness of this 'document' has been called into question (in my opinion, rightly). First, it must be admitted that Plutarch appears to be quoting from a documentary source which gave specific clauses in the decree and explicit procedures for its implementation ('twenty men were chosen . . . five of these . . .'). This source is generally held to have been the *Collection of Athenian Decrees* made by the Macedonian historian Craterus, whom Plutarch cites twice elsewhere, in the *Life of Aristeides* ch. 26 (= *FGH* 342 F 12) and the *Life of Cimon* ch. 13 (= 342 F 13, the problematic 'Peace of Callias,' to which we shall return). Inclusion of this 'document' in such a collection (which in any case remains a mere hypothesis) does not, of course, guarantee its authenticity.

The clause calling for discussion of 'the Greek sanctuaries which had been burnt down by the Persians' appears to touch on the alleged prohibition contained in the 'Oath of Plataea' (Diodorus 11.29.2; Lycurgus, *against Leocrates* 81), according to which the Greeks, assembled at the Isthmus of Corinth before the battle of Plataea in 479 B.C., swore 'not to rebuild any temple that has been burnt and destroyed . . . but let them be and leave them as a memorial to the sacrilege of the barbarians' (Meiggs, *The Athenian Empire* [Oxford, 1972] p. 504). That document itself has come under fire from scholars, and it is rather suspicious that the clause that prohibits rebuilding of the temples does not appear in the fourth-century inscription recording the oath, known as the 'Acharnae stele' (M.N. Tod, *A Selection of Greek Historical Inscriptions* vol. II [Oxford, 1948] no. 204, pp. 303-7; trans. in C.W. Fornara, *Archaic times to the end of the Peloponnesian War*, [2nd ed. Cambridge, 1983] no. 57, pp. 56-7). The implication of the clause in the 'Congress Decree' appears to be that now, for the first time since 479, the Greeks are to deliberate about rebuilding the shrines and holy places devastated by the Persians. It had been hoped that archaeology might establish an 'argument from silence', if it could be shown that no building in fact took place in Greece between (say) 480 and 450 B.C, but the evidence is ambiguous. See W.B. Broneer, *Hesperia* Suppl. 5 (1941) 156ff.; Meiggs, *Athenian Empire*, pp. 505-7.

It is not clear precisely to what the clause 'sacrifices owed to the gods on behalf of Hellas' refers, or what is the exact nature of the 'vows made when [the Greeks] were fighting the Persians'. The clause 'security of the seas, so that all ships could sail them without fear and keep the peace', together with Plutarch's reference later to 'deliberations for the peace and well-being of Greece', have been seen as allusions to the disputed 'Peace of Callias' which several ancient authorities, Plutarch among them (*Cimon* 13), assert was concluded between Athens and Persia. Quite apart from any purported connection with clauses in the 'Congress Decree', the 'Peace of Callias' itself continues to attract an undue amount of scholarly attention. As A. Andrewes wrote in 1981, 'The existence of the Peace of Kallias is still a matter of fierce controversy: there is perhaps no area of Greek history where more various propositions, many of them mutually contradictory, have been proclaimed as self-evident' (*A Historical Commentary on Thucydides* vol. V [Oxford, 1981] p. 135). There are two strong reasons for questioning the existence of such a Peace. It is not mentioned by Thucydides, even though the relevance to his account (even the summary account of the 'Pentecontaetia') of the growth of Athens' power and the increasingly oppressive control she exercised over her allies is obvious. Nor has it left a trace in any other fifth-century source. This point is well made by Stockton: '. . . the really disquieting thing is that the fifth century in fact offers no explicit evidence either for or against the Peace. Whatever the terms of the Peace are conjectured to have been, whether they were creditable to Athens or rather disappointing, it is remarkable that not one fifth-century authority should allude to it' ('The Peace of Callias', *Historia* 8 [1959] p. 64). Secondly, the inscription on which the Peace was recorded was denounced as a forgery by the fourth-century historians Theopompus (*FGH* 115 Ff 153-5) and Callisthenes (124 F 16). Plutarch tried to defend the authenticity of the 'Peace of Callias' on grounds that it was recorded in Craterus' *Athenian Decrees* (*Cimon* 13, referred to above), but in the same breath Plutarch appears to date it to the aftermath of Cimon's victory against the Persians and Phoenicians at the Euryedon River c. 469 B.C. (this chronology is also implied by Lycurgus, *against Leocrates* 73), a date which most scholars reject in favour of one twenty years later. An additional argument against the 'Peace of Callias' has been found in Plutarch's account in *Per.* 12 of the opposition Pericles had to face over the building program. Plutarch has his opponents (unnamed, but Thucydides son of Melesias is probably meant) object that Athens was 'gilding and beautifying' herself, 'as if it were some vain woman decking herself out with costly stones and statues and temples worth millions of money'—in other words, well after the building program that started in 448 had got under way—and Pericles is made to retort that 'the Athenians were not obliged to give the allies any account of how their money was spent, provided that they carried on the war for them and kept the Persians away.' Such an argument, as Stockton points out (pp. 69-70), would have been nonsensical if an actual peace treaty with Persia had already been concluded (see my note on chap. 12 above).

Recently A.J. Holladay put forward a compromise view: there was a peace, but it was 'unformalised', 'an agreement reached [by the Persian King] unofficially with an Athenian citizen [Kallias]'; 'Kallias' mission merely consisted of a statement of Pericles' intention to cease hostilities provided that Persia observed certain limits on her actions' (*Historia* 35 [1986] 505). This is a seductive hypothesis, but one could question the likelihood of such an arrangement when the Athenians normally placed such a premium on legalistic precision, with the minutiae of treaties and other official documents being spelled out in elaborate detail.

Gomme accepted the historicity of both the 'Peace of Callias' and the 'Congress Decree', and of the latter he wrote, 'the date of the proposed congress is quite uncertain, but 448 is probable, after the Peace of Kallias and immediately before the beginning of the building of the Parthenon' (*Commentary* vol. I, p. 367). But if that were so, why should one of the subjects to be discussed by the proposed Congress have been 'the security of the seas, so that all ships could sail them without fear and keep the peace'? The establishment of 'security of the seas' had been an important purpose of the Peace of Callias, by one of whose clauses (I quote from Plutarch's account in *Cimon* 13), the Persians agreed 'not to let a single warship or armoured vessel sail west of the Cyanean and the Chelidonian islands.'

Scholars who accept the authenticity of the 'Congress Decree' point to the clear and orderly procedure it sets forth for selecting twenty men 'above fifty years of age', a specification which appears once elsewhere, in a well-authenticated decree of 430 B.C. (R. Meiggs & D. Lewis, *A Selection of Greek Historical Inscriptions* [Oxford, 1969] no. 65, line 17 = S. Hornblower & M. Greenstock, *The Athenian Empire* LACTOR no. 1 [3rd ed., London, 1984] no. 159). It calls for these ambassadors to be sent, five to the Ionian and Dorian areas of the seaboard of Asia Minor and the islands, five to the Hellespont and Thrace, five to the Peloponnese and Acarnania, and the rest to the north-eastern part of the Greek mainland. As Meiggs remarks, 'there is a similar definition of routes in surviving fifth-century decrees [he gives examples]. . . . This is the only clause in Plutarch's account that is convincingly epigraphic' (*Athenian Empire*, 512). On the other hand, it has been noted that the first two regions named, 'Ionia' and 'the Hellespont', correspond to the first two of the five 'panels' under which Athens' tribute-paying allies were grouped for certain years in which the quotas were recorded on the 'Tribute Lists' (see Hornblower and Greenstock, *The Athenian Empire*, pp. 70-71).

Some who have challenged the Decree's authenticity have attempted to find an appropriate context in which it might have been forged. Two such possibilities have been suggested, in the 340s, as part of Athens' propaganda against Philip of Macedon (Seager), or in support of Philip's claim in the aftermath of his victory at Chaeronea in 338 B.C. to pose as *hegemon* of a united Greece in a 'holy crusade' against Persia (Bosworth). It needs to be stressed, however (a point I shall come back to in Endnote D, on the Megarian Decree), that critics need not feel obliged to find alternative contexts for details or episodes that may seem hard to justify in the places in which our ancient authorities report them, and, conversely, the discovery of a different and sometimes more appropriate setting for a document or narrative of events does not *ipso facto* prove that it belongs there. Each must stand (or fall) on its own merits. What makes the 'Congress Decree' particularly elusive, and perhaps puts it ultimately beyond criticism, is that it never came to fruition. It was a 'non-event', for, as Plutarch remarks in concluding his account, 'nothing was achieved, and the delegates never assembled because of the covert opposition of the Spartans.'

If we accept the authenticity of the Congress Decree, and roughly in the chronological position a consensus of modern scholars would put it, the early 440s, we must ask what Pericles was up to. As MacDonald has pointed out, 'the main thrust of the decree was political, not economic. By summoning the Congress, Athens was making a claim for leadership of all the Greeks' (*Historia* 31, 1982, 121). Can Pericles seriously have thought that the Spartans would send delegates and acquiesce in such a scheme? Or did he merely (as some scholars have suggested) wish to show them up as mean-spirited and uninterested in panhellenic ventures of this sort— especially if they were sponsored by and redounded to the glory of Athens? In that case, Plutarch is telling only half the story, and not the more important half at that, to record the episode simply as an illustration of Pericles' lofty spirit and of the grandeur of his conceptions.

Bibliography

('Congress Decree')

J.D. Smart, 'Perikles' Congress Decree,' unpublished lecture given in Ottawa, June 1967

R. Seager, 'The Congress Decree: some doubts and a hypothesis', *Historia* 18 (1969) 129-141

A.B. Bosworth, 'The Congress Decree: another hypothesis', *Historia* 20 (1971) 600-616

G.T. Griffith, 'A Note on Plutarch Pericles 17', *Historia* 27 (1978) 218-219

B. Macdonald, 'The Authenticity of the Congress Decree', *Historia* 31 (1982) 120-123

R. Meiggs, *The Athenian Empire* (Oxford, 1972) pp. 512-515

A.W. Gomme, *A Historical Commentary on Thucydides* vol. I (Oxford, 1945) pp. 366-367

('Peace of Callias')

C.W. Fornara, *Archaic Times to the End of the Peloponnesian War* (2nd ed. Cambridge, 1983) pp. 97-103

H.T. Wade-Gery, 'The Peace of Kallias', in *Harvard Studies in Classical Philology*, Suppl. 1 (1940) pp. 121-156 = *Essays in Greek History* (Oxford, 1958) pp. 201-232

A.W. Gomme, *A Historical Commentary on Thucydides* vol. I (Oxford, 1945) pp. 331-335

D. Stockton, 'The Peace of Callias', *Historia* 8 (1959) 61-79

S.K. Eddy, 'On the Peace of Callias', *Classical Philology* 65 (1970) 8-14

C.L. Murison, 'The Peace of Callias: its historical context', *Phoenix* 25 (1971) 12-31

G.E.M. de Ste. Croix, *The Origins of the Peloponnesian War* (London, 1972) Appendix VII

R. Meiggs, *The Athenian Empire* (Oxford, 1972) pp. 129-151, 487-495, 598-599

—— , rev. of K. Meister, *Die Ungeschichtlichkeit des Kalliasfriedens und ihren historischen Folgen* (Wiesbaden, 1982) in *Gnomon* 56 (1984) 35-38

A. Andrewes, *A Historical Commentary on Thucydides* vol. V (Oxford, 1981) p. 135

A.J. Holladay, 'The Détente of Kallias', *Historia* 35 (1986) 503-507

Endnote D *The Megarian Decree(s)*

Terms

It will be well to put out clearly the few undisputed facts regarding the so-called 'Megarian Decree'. At some time before the summer of 432 B.C., the Athenians passed a decree whose terms are summarized by Thucydides as follows: '[the Megarians] are debarred from using the harbours in the Athenian empire and the agora at Athens' (1.67.4). Gomme in his note *ad loc.* interpets the prohibition thus: 'they could neither buy nor sell in Attica, and they could not send their own ships into the harbours of the empire, though they might buy and sell there' (*Commentary* vol. I, p. 227). It is clear that, whenever the 'Decree against the Megarians' was originally passed—and, as we shall see, there is no way of knowing for certain whether this was a few months or several years earlier, it had become a cause célèbre. In the late summer and autumn of 432 the Spartans, having determined on their own to go to war with Athens and having secured approval for this action in a synod of their allies in the Peloponnesian League, sent a number of embassies to Athens to present the causes of complaint, among which the 'chief and clearest', according to Thucydides (1.139.1), was 'the decree about the Megarians' (here Thucydides explains it in almost precisely the same terms he had used at 1.67.4). The Athenians, he continues, were unwilling to yield on this point, 'charging in turn against the Megarians their encroachment upon land [at Eleusis] which was sacred and whose boundaries were unmarked, and the Megarians' reception of runaway slaves' (1.139.2).

What is not entirely clear, and what anyway does not affect the main point of this discussion, is whether these negotiations over Megara were serious. The way Thucydides tells the story, the Spartans had already voted for war in early summer 432, and had summoned their allies in the League merely to get them to rubber-stamp the decision. They decided to delay an actual declaration of war until they had had time to make the necessary preparations, and sent embassies to lay charges 'so that they would have the most plausible possible pretext for going to war, if the Athenians didn't comply' (1.126.1). This does make it look, in Thucydides' opinion at least, as though the Spartans' proposal 'that if [the Athenians] abrogated the Decree about the Megarians, there would not be war' (1.139.1), was merely a ploy. That was the way Pericles took it, at any rate, for Thucydides reports that the Athenians held an assembly to reply to the Spartans' offers 'once and for all'. There was a spirited debate, with some speakers calling for war and others again maintaining that 'the [Megarian] Decree not be an impediment to peace and should be repealed', to which Pericles retorted, 'Let no one suppose that we shall be going to war for a small matter, if we do not repeal the Megarian Decree . . . If you give way to them on this, they will soon be ordering you to do something more important, since you submitted to them on this out of fear' (1.140.4-5).

A satirical version of the Decree is given by Aristophanes, in the continuation of the passage from *Acharnians* from which Plutarch, at *Per.* 30, cites vv. 524-7:

And thereupon the beginning of the war broke out
for all Greeks, from — three prostitutes.
Thereupon angrily Pericles the Olympian
made lightning, made thunder, threw Greece into confusion,
and had laws passed that were written like drinking songs,
that Megarians 'must not stay on land or in agora
or on sea or in heaven.'   (vv. 528-534)

It is noteworthy that Aristophanes has left his imprint on one other detail of Plutarch's version of events. The passage from *Acharnians* continues with a description of the sequel to these events: 'thereupon the Megarians, since they were starving by inches, asked the Spartans to have the 'Decree about the Prostitutes' turned to the wall' (vv. 535-537). Plutarch's account in chap. 30 above, in which the ambassador's name is given as Polyalkes, is very similar.

How much stock are we to put in the remainder of chap. 30, which seems to derive (at least in part) ultimately from Thuc. 1.139.2 (quoted above), but with additional circumstantial details from another sourcePlutarch makes the following additions: a 'humane and reasonable' complaint against the Megarians for their encroachment upon the disputed sacred territory at Eleusis; the murder of the herald, Anthemocritus; the decree of Charinus declaring Athens an 'irreconcilable and implacable enemy' of Megara. The last point, at least, implacable enmity and twice-yearly invasions of the Megarid, is vouched for by Thucydides, who reports an invasion of Megara under Pericles in the autumn of 431 (2.31.1; cf. 4.66.1) and remarks that these devastations occurred until 424 B.C. (2.31.3). That the incident involving Anthemocritus did in fact occur seems to be guaranteed by Pausanias' report of a memorial statue in his honour set up by the Athenians just outside the Dipylon Gate along the 'Sacred Way' to Eleusis (1.36.3), and another ancient source which mentions the statue adds that the Athenians kept the Megarians from participating in the Eleusinian Mysteries as a punishment for murdering their herald.

On the other hand, some scholars have raised questions about the chronological and causal sequence of events implied by Plutarch's narrative. Is, for example, the 'humane and reasonable' complaint which Plutarch says Pericles lodged against the Megarians for cultivating sacred ground at Eleusis to be identified with, or was it at least directly antecedent to, the decree excluding Megara from trade in the Athenian Empire and from the marketplace at Athens? One would suppose so, in light of the similar wording used by Plutarch and Thucydides regarding the Megarians' appropriation of the disputed land at Eleusis. It should be noted, however, that Plutarch's narrative introduces an additional stage, for Thucydides' description of the course of events certainly does not mention, does not even hint at, a gradual escalation of anger against Megara. On the contrary, so far from leaving room for a 'humane and reasonable' protest, Thucydides implies that the Athenians' response to Megara's encroachments at Eleusis was immediately and in the first instance the rather drastic one of excluding Megara from all trade with Athens. Secondly, Plutarch's account of the slaying of Anthemocritus and the decree of Charinus also makes an ill fit with Thucydides' narrative, in which no mention at all is made of direct diplomatic negotiations between Athens and Megara. And yet, since (as we have seen), Thucydides attests the twice-yearly invasions, which logically presuppose some more violent misdeed against Athens than the contretemps over Eleusis (for, on the hypothesis, the 'Megarian Decree' excluding them from trade was a reprisal for that offense), Thucydides seems tacitly to recognize something like Plutarch's sequence of events.

One could sketch a hypothetical sequence of events which took into account the various stages in the worsening relations between Athens and Megara, as follows: (1) Megara encroaches on land at Eleusis claimed by Athens to be sacred, and is also allegedly harbouring runaway Athenian slaves; (2) Athens responds with the 'Megarian Decree' prohibiting all Megarian trade, both at Athens itself and in the ports of the empire; (3) because Megara does not desist from her alleged desecrations at Eleusis, Pericles proposes the sending of Anthemocritus to make a further pointed, yet at the same time 'humane and reasonable', complaint (so described by later writers in contrast to the much more severe stage to follow); (4) Anthemocritus is killed, perhaps by an angry mob of Megarian 'toughs,' and Athens responds with the more brutal decree of Charinus, declaring 'eternal enmity' between the two cities and calling for summary execution of any Megarian found on Attic soil and for twice yearly invasions of Megarian territory by Athenian generals.

Finally, a word needs to be said about attempts to move the events in *Per.* 30, including Anthemocritus and Charinus, down to the mid-fourth century. Fortunately, this scissors-and-paste approach to the ancient sources is not so much in fashion today as it was (say) ten or fifteen years ago. Doubtless various historical contexts could be found into which not only this, but other episodes reported from the fifth century might be made to fit (for example, the 'Congress Decree'; see Endnote C). But no purpose is served by wholesale rearrangements of this kind, and it is no mark against the historicity of an account to find another, and perhaps (in the eyes of some critics) likelier setting for it. Plutarch's narrative in chap. 30, though not without some problematic aspects, should be left where he placed it, and judged believable or not on its own merits.

Date and Significance

Thucydides' extended narrative of 'the Corcyra affair' includes a full-scale debate, ostensibly held in about June 433 B.C., in which a Corinthian speaker at Athens, besides trying to dissuade the Athenians from undertaking a destabilizing alliance with the Corinthian colony of Corcyra, tells his audience to 'remove the previously existing suspicion about Megara' (1.42.2). This sentence has been subjected to a great deal of scholarly scrutiny and, although some would disagree, I feel with Gomme that 'there is much to be said for Steup's view that Thucydides is here referring to a more recent suspicion aroused by those Athenian measures against Megara which culminated in her exclusion from all the ports of the empire' (*Commentary* vol. I, p. 175). If this is correct, the exclusion decree will have been passed by spring 433 (indeed, Brunt would put it some years before that), although a majority opinion places it rather nearer to the events narrated by Thucydides as having occurred in the summer of 432.

The decree must have been intended to hurt the Megarians economically, as well as being a humiliating insult and a frustration to them diplomatically on the international Greek scene. De Ste. Croix tries to play down the economic impact by pointing out (quite correctly) that we have no way of gauging the degree of hurt inflicted on the Megarian economy, and he remarks that account is not generally taken of the possibility that some Megarian trade was carried in ships of other Greek states, who would, of course, not have been debarred from using Athenian-controlled ports. Both these points are true. But it seems to me to fly in the face of the obvious to ignore the devastating effect that exclusion from direct trading activity would have had on a country that (so far as we can tell) earned most of her national income from trade. The main character ᵗⁿ *Acharnians* makes sport of the excessively zealous denunciation of those who attempted to deal in such trivial items as 'Megarian little cloaks . . . cucumber or little hare or little pig or garlic or lumps of salt' (vv. 519ff.; cf. vv. 818ff. As Hornblower remarks with reference to this passage, 'an elaborate parody of the Megarian decree is *immediately* followed by the statement that the Megarians were starving slowly [v.535]' (*The Greek World*, 479-323 B.C. [London and New York, 1983] p. 92; so, too, Fornara, *Yale Classical Studies* 24 (1975) pp. 225-6). Later in the play, in the humorous but at the same time painfully pathetic scene in which the starving Megarian appears and tries to sell his daughters disguised as pigs (vv. 729-835), the audience was no doubt meant to laugh at the man's plight, but behind the laughter there was also (as often) a barb: was the 'Education of Hellas' prepared to reduce her enemies to this? Admittedly, the emphasis in this latter scene is on the devastation wrought by the twice-yearly invasions (vv. 761-2). But, to adapt an argument of Hornblower's, it is 'perverse' to dissociate the effects of Athens' two moves against Megara, the exclusion decree and the invasions, and to 'insist [as de Ste. Croix attempts to do] that the starvation refers to routine annual invasions of the Megarid' (*ibid.*). The cumulative effect of years of being denied access to direct trade with Athens must be at least part of the reason the Megarians are in the sorry state that Aristophanes was milking for laughs in 425 B.C. As the Megarian says when Dikaiopolis—is there a touch of irony in Aristophanes' choice of this name for his Athenian hero, 'Citizen of a Just City'?—salutes him in parting with the usual phrase, 'Fare you well', 'That (i.e., faring well) is not one of Megara's local specialities' (v. 832).

Bibliography

R.J. Bonner, 'The Megarian Decrees', *Classical Philology* 16 (1921) 238-245

P.A. Brunt, 'The Megarian Decree,' *American Journal of Philology* 72 (1951) 269-282

W.R. Connor, 'Charinus' Megarian Decree', *AJP* [above] 83 (1962) 225-246

K.J. Dover, 'Anthemocritus and the Megarians', *AJP* 87 (1966) 203-209

L.J. Bliquez, 'Anthemocritus and the *orgas* disputes', *Greek, Roman & Byzantine Studies* 10 (1969) 157-161

G.L. Cawkwell, 'Anthemocritus and the Megarians and the decree of Charinus', *Revue des études grecques* 82 (1969) 327-335

G.E.M. de Ste. Croix, *The Origins of the Peloponnesian War* (London: Duckworth, 1972) ch. VI, pp. 225ff., with App. xxxvii, pp. 386ff

R. Meiggs, *The Athenian Empire* (Oxford, 1972) pp. 430-431

C.W. Fornara, 'Plutarch and the Megarian Decree', *Yale Classical Studies* 24 (1975) 213-228

A. French, 'The Megarian Decree', *Historia* 25 (1976) 245-249

C. Tuplin, 'Thuc. I.42.2 and the Megarian Decree', *Classical Quarterly* 29 (1979) 301-307

B.R. MacDonald, 'The Megarian Decree', *Historia* 32 (1983) 385-410

P.A. Stadter, 'Plutarch, Charinus and the Megarian Decree', *GRBS* [above] 25 (1984) 351-372

Endnote E *Anaxagoras' Dates and the Attacks on Pericles*

It was pointed out in the notes to chap. 32 above that there were varying accounts of how Pericles contrived to shelter Anaxagoras from Diopeithes' decree against impiety. The version Plutarch follows there is that Pericles 'was so alarmed for Anaxagoras' safety that he smuggled him out of the city', although at *Nicias* 23 we read that 'Anaxagoras was imprisoned, till Pericles managed to rescue him with great difficulty.' Whichever account is to be preferred, the implication is that Diopeithes' decree and Anaxagoras' subsequent prosecution under its terms, like the alleged trial of Aspasia and the charges against Pheidias, are to be dated to the period just before the outbreak of the Peloponnesian War. It is disquieting, then, to find that some of the evidence for Anaxagoras' dates makes this chronology impossible. Diogenes Laertius, writing *Lives of the Philosophers* in the third century A.D., cites earlier chronographic sources about Anaxagoras, not all of them, it must be admitted, internally consistent or reconcilable one with another (Diog. Laert. II.7: see Kirk, Raven & Scholfield pp. 352-3). On the chronographer Apollodorus' testimony (2nd century B.C.), Anaxagoras was born about 500 B.C. and died (emending the numeral) in 428/7; these are the dates generally accepted by scholars for his lifespan. Another source, Demeterius of Phaleron (see Intro., sec. 3), reports that he was active as a philosopher at Athens for 30 years. With a 'correction' of Demetrius' archon-year for the beginning of the thirty-year period, the dates will be 480—Demeterius noted that Anaxagoras was twenty at the beginning of the period—to 450 B.C. This early chronology seems to fit with the testimony of Satyrus (see Intro., sec. 3) that he was prosecuted by Thucydides son of Melesias as part of the latter's political attacks against Pericles. Satyrus also said that the charge brought against him was 'not only impiety [as Plutarch and other sources imply], but Medism', that is, collaboration with, or favouring the interests of, the Persians. In support of this chronological scheme, historians of philosophy note that the biographical tradition about Socrates never brought the two men into face-to-face contact as contemporaries, but on the contrary implied that Anaxagoras was of an older philosophical generation than Socrates (some made Anaxagoras the teacher of Socrates, although the usual view was that Socrates was taught by Archelaos, himself a pupil of Anaxagoras). On this chronology, the story of how Pericles came to Anaxagoras' rescue must either be transferred to c. 450 B.C., or be declared pure fiction, a conclusion perhaps not out of keeping with the highly romanticized and mutually inconsistent reports of Pericles' role in the affair.

On the other side, there is the chronology clearly implied by

Plutarch's account, which appears to go back to Ephorus (cf. Diodorus 12.39.2). Moreover, some of the anecdotes connecting Anaxagoras with Pericles (like that at the end of chap. 16) suggest a close and continuing connection between the two men beyond the period of Pericles' youth and formative years, and well into a time when, as Plutarch says there, "Pericles was absorbed in public affairs". And alternative names of Anaxagoras' prosecutor were given: Cleon (reported by Sotion; see note on chap. 32), or the name that Plutarch himself offers, Diopeithes. The activity of either of these fits more easily into the period just before 431 than c. 450 B.C. I am inclined to accept this 'late' chronology, even though it requires rejection of the tradition that Anaxagoras came to Athens from Clazomenae because of the disruption in Ionia caused by Xerxes' expedition, and the report of a thirty-year period of philosophical activity at Athens must be abandoned, for it is unsound method to say that 'it could represent the sum total of his stays in Athens' (Meiggs, *Athenian Empire*, p. 438; so, too, Guthrie, *History of Greek Philosophy* vol. II, p. 323).

Mansfeld (*Mnemosyne* 4th ser. [1979] pp. 39ff.) attempts to harmonize the conflicting chronological testimonies as follows: Anaxagoras born 499/8 and died, aged 72, in 428/7, from Apollodorus, the second centrury B.C. Athenian chronographer; came to Athens and started his career as a philosopher in 456/5 ('the year of Callias', from Demetrius of Phaleron, *Record of Athenian Archons*, unemended); stayed at Athens 20 years (Demetrius, emended), which would make the year of his trial 437/6. This reconstruction, however, ignores the tradition that Anaxagoras' Athenian period was reported as having lasted 30, not 20 years, and it fails to take account of the strong implication in Plutarch's narrative that the attacks against Anaxagoras were just part of a larger barrage against Pericles that was mounted by his enemies to assail his position of pre-eminence on the eve of the war.

Whatever the truth about the date and circumstances of Anaxagoras' departure from Athens, there was a credible tradition that he lived out his last years in Lampsacus, where he was given honourable burial and where a commemorative school holiday was celebrated in his memory down to Diogenes Laertius' own day (II.14; confirmed by the fourth-century rhetorician Alcidamas, whom Aristotle cites at *Rhetoric* 1398 b 10).

In chap. 32 Plutarch also gives an account of a trial of Aspasia, who was allegedly prosecuted by the comic poet Hermippus on a charge of impiety. All of this seems to me extremely questionable. It is one thing to accept that philosophers like Anaxagoras, Protagoras and Socrates were open to prosecution for their unorthodox teachings, quite another to see how such a charge could ever have been made to appear plausible against Pericles' mistress. I prefer to follow those who see here a misinterpretation of a scene from some comedy, by Hermippus or someone else, in which she was ridiculed for encouraging Pericles to let Athens be 'infected' by new ideas. Some such comic travesty may also lie behind the stories of how Aspasia initiated Pericles into the art of oratory and even—like some kind of real-life Diotima—Socrates into various arcane refinements of the 'higher learning' (see notes on chap. 24).

There are real, perhaps insuperable, difficulties concerning the trial of Pheidias as well. As Plutarch tells the story in chap. 31, one of Pheidias' associates, a certain Menon, was suborned by Pericles' enemies to lay a charge of embezzlement against the sculptor in connection with the gold plate on the Parthenos statue; the alleged portrait-likenesses of himself and Pericles on Athena's shield are mentioned as a contributing cause of the people's 'jealousy' against Pheidias, but these formed no part (apparently) of the formal indictment. Pericles countered by having the gold plates removed from the statue and weighed, with the result that the prosecutors were discredited. In the meantime, however, according to Plutarch, Pheidias, still imprisoned, "fell sick and died". Although Plutarch gives no specific indication of the date of this alleged prosecution of Pheidias, his narrative of it in connection with the 'Megarian Decree' and as part of the run-up to the outbreak of the war suggests a date c. 432 B.C. Another version is reported, that of Philochorus (*FGH* 328 F 121), which, although some alteration of archon-names is required to bring about internal consistency, appears to date the trial to 438/7, immediately after the completion of the statue. The charge is here reported to have been laid in respect of the ivory, or the gold and the ivory, used for the scales of the serpent coiled inside Athena's shield. We are told that Pheidias was tried and condemned to exile, which he spent in Elis; there he undertook the colossal statue of Olympian Zeus (see chap. 2), but was once again charged by his patrons with embezzlement, condemned to death and executed. Several details here call for incredulity: uncertainty whether the snake's scales, funds for which Pheidias allegedly misappropriated, were of gold or ivory, and the very suspicious duplication of trials— and on similar charges—at Elis and Athens. If, however, we overlook these discrepancies, Philochorus' chronology seems to be incompatible with that implied by Plutarch, who appears to date this attack on Pheidias, along with the others, on the eve of the outbreak of war (the irreconcilability of dates is also noted by the Scholiast on Aristophanes' *Peace* 605, a passage cited in Endnote A, who is our source for the testimony by Philochorus).

I can think of only one way of reconciling Philochorus and Plutarch. We might suppose that Dracontides' bill mentioned in chap. 32, which, according to Plutarch, directed that "the accounts of the public funds that Pericles had spent should be deposited with the prytanes," somehow involved resuscitation of charges brought originally against Pheidias in 438/7. Some confirmation for this suggestion might be sought in Plutarch's rather cryptic comment later in chap. 32, that "Pericles had already fallen foul of the people on the occasion of Pheidias' trial and he dreaded the jury's verdict in his own case," and consequently "deliberately fanned [the war] into flame," using the Megarian Decree as a smokescreen. But such contortions are perhaps not preferable to simply choosing between Philochorus' chronology for Pheidias' trial and that implied by Plutarch, which may itself, however, rest on nothing more substantial than, as was pointed out in Endnote A, a misunderstanding (by Ephorus?) of a joke in Aristophanes.

Bibliography

A.E. Taylor, 'On the Date of the Trial of Anaxagoras', *Classical Quarterly* 11 (1917) 81-87

J. Burnet, *Early Greek Philosophy* (4th. ed. London, 1930; reprinted) 252-252

J.A. Davison, 'Protagoras, Democritus and Anaxagoras', *CQ* [above] 47 (1953) 33-45

A.W. Gomme, *A Historical Commentary on Thucydides* vol. II (Oxford, 1956) 184-189

F.J. Frost, 'Pericles and Dracontides', *Journal of Hellenic Studies* 84 (1964) 69-72

W.K.C. Guthrie, *A History of Greek Philosophy* vol. II (Cambridge, 1965) pp. 322-323

R. Meiggs, *The Athenian Empire* (Oxford, 1972) 435-436

K.J. Dover, 'The Freedom of the Intellectual in Greek Society', *Talanta* 7 (1975) 24-54 esp. 27-34, 39-41

A. Andrewes, 'The Opposition to Perikles', *JHS* [above] 108 (1978) 1-8

J. Mansfeld, 'The Chronology of Anaxagoras' Athenian Period and the Date of his Trial', *Mnemosyne* 4th ser. 32 (1979) 39-60; 33 (1980) 17-95

D. Sider, *The Fragments of Aristophanes* (Meisenheim am Glan, 1981) pp. 1-11

L. Woodbury, 'Anaxagoras and Athens', *Phoenix* 35 (1981) 295-315

G.S. Kirk, J.E. Raven and M. Schofield, *The Presocratic Philosophers* (2nd ed. Cambridge, 1983) pp. 352-355

Endnote F   *The Family of Pericles* (see page 26)

Pericles was born in the mid to late 490s. (It is sometimes maintained that he would have to have been at least twenty to be choregus for Aeschylus' *Persians* in 472 B.C., but I know of no evidence for this. If there is any basis to Plutarch's report at *Cimon* 13—apparently citing Callisthenes—that Pericles shared a naval command with Ephialtes in the eastern Aegean, Pericles will have been at least thirty on that occasion, no later than the late 460s.) On his mother's side he was an Alcmeonid, for she was Agariste, niece of the lawgiver Cleisthenes, whose mother was an earlier Agariste, wife of the Athenian Megacles and daughter of the tyrant of Sicyon. Pericles' uncle, also a Megacles, was ostracized in 486 B.C. for alleged connections with the family of Athens' deposed tyrants, the Peisistratids. By a twist of archaeological fate, '4,662 ostraca bearing [this almost unknown Megacles'] name have been found, more than for any other man' (Rhodes, *Commentary on the Aristotelian Athenaion Politeia*, p. 275). It is probably this same Megacles who, while in exile, won a four-horse-chariot victory at Delphi's Pythian Games and commissioned Pindar's *Seventh Pythian* ode.

From his father's family, too, Pericles might easily have acquired an interest in public life. The name of his paternal grandfather, Ariphron, appears in a philosophical dialogue preserved on a third century A.D. papyrus (*P. Oxy.* 664), but which probably goes back to some follower of Aristotle in the Peripatetic School (see Intro., sec. 3). The topic of the dialogue is government, more specifically, the reign of the Corinthian tyrant, Periander. Among the speakers are Ariphron (almost certainly to be identified as Pericles' grandfather) and the Athenian tyrant, Peisistratus. (From this it has been inferred that Ariphron was a 'partisan' or 'courtier' of the Peisistratids, but the writer of the dialogue may simply be writing authentic-sounding fiction by bringing together, quite unhistorically, well-known names from the sixth century B.C. It is in any case difficult to see how any of these men in their prime could have been contemporary with Periander.)

Pericles' father was Xanthippus, who was one of Athens' leading politicians in the 480s. He is first named as prosecutor of the general Miltiades after the latter's abortive campaign against Paros c. 489 B.C. (Herodotus 6.136). He was ostracized two years after Megacles, in 484 B.C., and one ostrakon adds an extra bit of abuse, saying that he 'does most wrong of all the accursed leaders.' In a rather cryptic reference in the *Constitution of Athens* (28.2) he is mentioned in a list of leaders of the popular party; in what appears to be a chronological sequence, he is said to have held the post before Themistocles and to have had Miltiades as his aristocratic opponent; the assertion may be based on nothing more substantial than the prosecution after Paros, already mentioned.

Xanthippus was among those recalled on Themistocles' initiative before Salamis. An anecdote during the evacuation of the city is recounted by Plutarch at *Them*. 10: Xanthippus' faithful dog swam across to the island to join its master, only to die from the effort, in a kind of pale imitation of Odysseus' dog Argos. He is named in a list of ambassadors to Sparta in the spring of 479 B.C. to seek help against Mardonius' Persian force, and he commanded the Athenian troops at the battle of Mt. Mycale in the autumn of that year. The following winter he led the Athenians and their new Ionian allies in a siege of an enclave of Persians at Sestos on the Hellespont. The city was captured in the spring of 478 and Xanthippus was remembered for his stern, but perhaps justified, treatment of the governor of the place. In a rather confused narrative, Diodorus (11.42) names him along with Aristeides as intermediaries between Themistocles and the Athenian Assembly in the matter of completing the fortifications of Peiraeus, a project which Thucydides (1.93) says Themistocles undertook after finishing the city walls. Xanthippus' name is mentioned fleetingly in a poem by the contemporary Timocreon of Rhodes (fr. 727 Page, from Plutarch, *Them*. 21) and Pausanias reports (1.25.1) that, like his son Pericles, he was honoured by a commemorative statue on the Acropolis.

Pericles had a brother, probably older than he, since he was named Ariphron after his paternal grandfather. The two became joint guardians of their kinsmen, Alcibiades and Cleinias, after the boys' father was killed at the battle of Coroneia in 447 B.C. Alcibiades is called Pericles' 'nephew' in some ancient sources, but this cannot be correct; his mother, Deinomache, and Pericles were first cousins. Since Alcibiades was born c. 451 B.C., he will have been only in his late 'teens at the time of the anecdote related by Plutarch in chap. 37 (if that has any basis in fact).

Pericles also had a sister, of whom nothing is known beyond the fact that she died in the plague (chap. 36).

Pericles had two legitimate sons, the elder named for Pericles' father, Xanthippus, and the younger bearing the remarkable name of one of Athens' two state galleys, Paralos. On the likeliest scheme for reconstructing the sequence of his mother's marriages and her other offspring (see below), Xanthippus will have been about 23 at the time of his death in the plague. The anecdotes about Pericles and his daughter-in-law (chaps. 13 and 36) show that the boy married at an unusually early age. Paralos is mentioned by name, and hence was probably already an adult, in the 'Springhouse Decree' (see n. on chap. 24 and Endnote B). When the plague deprived Pericles of legitimate offspring, he was forced to seek dispensation from his own citizenship law in behalf of his son by Aspasia, the younger Pericles (chap. 37).

The sequence of Pericles' wife's marriages is a vexed topic.

Plutarch, our only authority to give specific information on the subject, states that she was married first to Hipponicus, next to Pericles, and finally to a third individual, a match which Pericles himself helped to arrange (chap. 24). Although Plutarch's testimony has often been challenged (by Blass, Beloch and, more recently, J.K. Davies), he has had several defenders among recent scholars. What counts most against Plutarch is the fact that the lady's son by Hipponicus, Callias who was nicknamed 'the Wealthy', a man who achieved notoriety as a butt of jests on the comic stage for his dissolute lifestyle, was still living in 367 B.C. If Plutarch's chronology is correct, he will have been just short of ninety. On the other hand, the alternative chronology would make him only ten years younger, and an active eighty-year-old is itself a statistical improbability.

Although Plutarch does not give the name of Pericles' wife, he provides the information that she was "closely related to him". Now it is known that Alcibiades' mother, Deinomache, was Pericles' first cousin, since her father, the Megacles ostracised in 486, was the brother of Pericles' mother, Agariste. It is tempting to follow Cromey in identifying Deinomache also as Pericles' wife, whom he divorced in the late 450s. If that is correct, Alcibiades was not only Pericles' *anepsiadous*, 'first cousin's son', but also — in a sense — his stepson, as he is designated by Nepos. For those who find it 'impossible' or at least unlikely that the striking fact of Alcibiades' mother's marriage to Pericles before she married Cleinias eluded or was ignored by the sources which Plutarch used, a modification of the theory would make Pericles' wife not Deinomache herself, but an unnamed sister of Deinomache (Thompson). The family-tree appended here accepts the first hypothesis, that Pericles' wife was the lady who later became Alcibiades' mother, Deinomache.

The younger Pericles, his illegitimate son by Aspasia, led a fairly active public life at Athens after his father's death. He was elected as *Hellenotamias*, Treasurer of the Empire, in 410/9 which, as Davies remarks, 'implies that he was born by 440'. He was on the board of ten generals elected in the spring of 406 after Alcibiades' débâcle at Notium. After a victory against the Spartans near the Arginusae ιslands, off Mytilene, in the summer of that year, he and five colleagues were arrested on a charge of gross negligence in failing to supervise the rescue of survivors from the ships that had been sunk in the battle. In spite of a spirited defense by his kinsman Euryptolemus (probably a relative, but it is not certain in what degree of kinship, to the Euryptolemus mentioned in *Per.* chap. 7; see Davies, *Athenian Propertied Families* pp. 377-8), he with the others was tried by an illegal, because collective, judicial proceeding and executed (chap. 37 above).

Nothing further is heard of any direct descendants of Pericles.

Bibliography

J.K. Davies, *Athenian Propertied Families* 600-300 B.C. (Oxford, 1971) pp. 262-263, 455-460

Robert D. Cromey, 'Perikles' Wife: chronological considerations', *Greek, Roman & Byzantine Studies* 23 (1982) 203-212

—— , 'On Deinomache', *Historia* 33 (1984) 385-401

P.J. Bicknell, 'Axiochos Alkibiadou, Aspasia and Aspasios', *L'antiquité classique* 51 (1982) 240-250

W.E. Thompson, 'The Kinship of Perikles and Alkibiades', *GRBS* [above] 11 (1970) 27-33